StartupNation

StartupNation

America's Leading
Entrepreneurial
Experts Reveal the
Secrets to Building
a Blockbuster
Business

JEFF SLOAN AND RICH SLOAN

CURRENCY

DOUBLEDAY

NEW YORK   LONDON   TORONTO   SYDNEY   AUCKLAND

A CURRENCY BOOK
PUBLISHED BY DOUBLEDAY
a division of Random House, Inc.

CURRENCY is a trademark of Random House, Inc., and
DOUBLEDAY is a registered trademark of Random House, Inc.

Grateful acknowledgment is made to reprint "The Stonecutter," from
The Tao of Pooh by Benjamin Hoff, copyright © 1982 by Benjamin Hoff.
Used by permission of Dutton, a division of Penguin Group (USA) Inc.

Library of Congress Cataloging-in-Publication Data
Sloan, Jeff.
StartupNation : America's leading entrepreneurial experts reveal the secrets
to building a blockbuster business / by Jeff Sloan and Rich Sloan.—1st ed.
p. cm.
1. New business enterprises—United States. 2. Entrepreneurship—
United States. I. Sloan, Rich. II. Title.
HD62.5.S576 2005
658.1'1—dc22
2004065547

ISBN 0-385-51248-1

Book design by Chris Welch
Photo credit: Steve Kovich

PRINTED IN THE UNITED STATES OF AMERICA

First Edition: June 2005

SPECIAL SALES
Currency Books are available at special discounts for bulk purchases for sales
promotions or premiums. Special editions, including personalized covers,
excerpts of existing books, and corporate imprints, can be created in large
quantities for special needs. For more information, write to Special Markets,
Currency Books, specialmarkets@randomhouse.com.

5 7 9 10 8 6

To Mom and Dad, our sister Julie,
and our grandfather Sam—a true entrepreneur

Contents

John Auman, Lisa Bailey, Tom Bailey, Hector Barreto, Mike Beauregard, Christine Beck, Matt Berenson, Fred Beyerlein, Rip Beyman, Susan Bidel, Richard Blouse, Bo, Bill Bowen, Foster Braun, Mike Brennan, George Brewer, Norm and Elaine Brodsky, Carolyn Buchanan, Chris Cameron, Francois Castaing, Laura Castaing, Anne Cole, Michael Colone, Dan Cherrin, Brian Cleveland, Katharine Cluverius, Heather Cohen, David Cole, Clark Collins, Josh Corn, Tom and Kathy Crum, Meagan Darlington, Terry Dauod, Tom Demay, Geoff Dodge, Tami Door, David Drake, Brian Dumaine, Michael Egren, Phillip Elkus, Fred Erb, Gary Erickson, Lia Ervans, Mike Fezzey, Andrew Field, Doug Fieldhouse, Phillip and Lauren Fisher, Ed Fleckenstein, Dan Fleckenstein, Mark Fortier, Pete Franco, Stanley Frankel, Chuck Fuller, Allyson Gabrys, Dawn Gatlin, Al and Ruth Glancy, Lynn Goldberg, Sara Gozmanian, Todd Graham, Jennifer Granholm, Eric Granowicz, Ray Gunn, Merle Harris, Reyn Hendrickson, Frank and Carol Hennessey, Barbara Henricks, David Hermelin, Carrie Himelfarb, Marvin Himelfarb, Chris Hoffman, Rich Homberg, Jonathan Hudson,

Rick Inatome, Joan Isabella, Kaye Ishee, Stephanie Jacobson, Ira Jaffe, JD, Gregg Johnson, Herb Kaufman, Kraig Kitchin, Kay and Billy Koplovitz, Steve Kovich, Van Lai, John Langmore, Hannan Lis, Dana Locniskar, Lyric, Bill MacArthur, Mike MacDougal, Vladimir Makorov, Florine Mark, Lou Merz, Eugene Miller, Tony Modafferi, Josh Mondry, Mitch Mondry, Mark and Betty Morris, Steve Mowat, Dan Mulhern, Cindi Murch, Ed Nakfoor, Ed Narens, Rich Nawrocki, Marci Nussbaum, Deanna Oppenheimer, Julia Parrish, Andy Pascal, Delia Passi, Ken Paulus, Bruce Perlmutter, Ben Permut, Jac Pierce, Lowell Potiker, Joe Ragnone, Steve Reed, Jennifer Reingold, Jennifer Reitman, Melanie Rembrandt, Eric Rix, Morrie Rochlin, Dion Roddy, Rich Rogel, Matt Roush, Paul Roy, Melanie Sabelhouse, Brandy Saigh, Victor Saroki, Jessica Schlick, Roger Scholl, David Schostak, Howard Schultz, Shahin, David Sherman, Diana Sikes, John Siverling, Patsy Smith, Sheldon Smith, Nicole Summitt, Danielle Susser, Alan Sussman, Hal and Dorothy Thau, Jim Tisdel, Eric Toler, Karen Torres, Sam Valenti, Christy VandenBosch, Roger VanDerSnick, Chad Warner, Joel Welsh, Jeff Weiss, Mike Wendland, Bill Wetsman, David Wetsman, Dave Wight, Ann Wilderom, Hugh Wiley, The Ray H. Witt family, Cathy Wolford, Paul Zlotoff.

A mission as important as ours requires superstar people to bring it to life. We're inspired every day by the passion, creativity, and commitment of the stars around us—our team members, our mentors, our friends, and our partners.

You've always encouraged us, faithfully guided us, and helped us achieve more in less time than we ever thought possible.

Thank You

We are profoundly grateful.

Introduction

You're a dreamer, right? That's why you've picked up this book. Maybe you've had a great idea knocking around inside your head for years. Maybe you've roughed it out on the back of a napkin and tucked it away somewhere. But you don't know what the next step is or what the *first* step is. Or, just maybe, you're sitting in your cubicle, next to a hundred other cubicles, thinking, "How do I stop workin' for the man?" If any of these descriptions fit you, you're an entrepreneur-in-waiting. And you're not alone. You're one of us—one of the two-thirds of Americans who dream about owning their own business.

This book is filled with "show and tell," designed to *show* you how your fellow entrepreneurs have been successful and *tell* you exactly what key moves you should make to position yourself for your own success. If we—the Sloan brothers—achieve our goal, the pages ahead will jump to life with real-world, in-the-trenches wisdom that will move you to action and inspire you to join up with a nation of extraordinary people doing extraordinary things.

Striking out on your own, doing your own thing—it's in our collective American blood. It's the very soul of our nation's economy. That's what we believe. This drive goes all the way back to those first pioneers who looked at the Atlantic and thought, "I wonder what I could do over there?" They reached the shores of America, then the Appalachians, the Mississippi River, the Rocky Mountains, and just kept going until America was a coast-to-coast dreamland for people seeking to lead a better life.

It's the spirit of those pioneers and all of the innovative entrepreneurs since then that have made the United States so prosperous. After all, this is a place where you can work hard to create something of your own, follow through on your dream, and have the freedom to decide what course your life will take. Nowhere else in the world is freedom and opportunity so woven into the fabric of a national identity. And we believe owning your own business is an integral part of this freedom.

The entrepreneurial roots run deep in America. They stretch back at least as far as individuals like Benjamin Franklin, who exemplifies how business and American democracy are so intertwined. Franklin, who first said "Early to bed and early to rise makes a man healthy, wealthy and wise," went on to contribute to the writing of the Declaration of Independence, in which he embraced the principle that a very essential individual freedom was owning one's own business.

At the turn of the twentieth century, this entrepreneurial spirit reached a peak in our home state of Michigan, the place where the automotive industry grew into a global giant. But it started out as a series of smaller entrepreneurial successes. Michigan is where Dodge and Chrysler first put their names on cars. Flint, the town where we grew up, is where General Motors set down many of its roots, pumping out millions of cars from factories right near our home. Down the road, in Dearborn, is where Henry Ford built the famous Rouge plant that took in steel, coal, and glass at one end and turned out Model Ts at the other end. Most people today think of Henry Ford as one of the world's greatest industrialists. But during the startup boom of the early 1900s, he was one of the world's greatest entrepreneurs.

Today, entrepreneurship is as vital and strong as ever. We're not talking about the entrepreneurship represented by the high-tech "boom" of the nineties, a run of startups based on hyped-up projections for growth. What we mean is the long-sustained growth of businesses built on time-tested fundamentals like the ones that contributed to making our country into the global economic powerhouse it is today.

So vast is the United States' small-business economy that it is greater than the *total* economies of France, Germany, and Great Britain *put together*. Small businesses today account for 51 percent of the American GDP and 99 percent of all employers, and creates 75 percent of all new jobs.

Beyond these powerful statistics, though, we believe that business ownership can transform individuals' lives. We've become convinced of this through our own entrepreneurial experience and by talking with and e-mailing thousands of entrepreneurs whom we've coached over the years. Whether it's via our weekly StartupNation radio show, our online seminar series, our tele-coaching calls, or our live events, we're more confident than ever that entrepreneurship is alive and well, even in spite of the burst of the dot-com bubble, the subsequent recession, and the ongoing global political uncertainty. We hear from entrepreneurs all over the globe who hunger for advice on how to get started, how to successfully grow their businesses, and how to use the power of entrepreneurship and business ownership to create the life they've always dreamed of.

That's what this book, *StartupNation,* is all about. It's about creating a business that sets in motion the life you want to lead. It's about giving you the inspiration and information you need to take your idea and turn it into reality *today*. It's about the passion and drive to turn breakthrough ideas, thought up by everyday people, into thriving companies. It's about being your own boss and relishing that life of freedom. But it's also about the nitty-gritty of business basics like managing cash flow, writing a solid business plan, and hiring great people so that your idea will have the best odds for success.

In the chapters to come, you'll learn about entrepreneurs who've embraced and applied the principles we live by. They work on Main Streets across America just like the one where we work in Birmingham, Michigan.

Our Main Street is called "Old Woodward Avenue." Our office is neighbored by dozens of other businesses, each one adding energy and passion to our community. These businesses create the connective tissue that brings people from around the world together to provide goods and services, conduct commerce, and build satisfying lives for themselves.

Down the street from us there's "Miss Kate," a funky women's retail clothing boutique owned by twenty-something Kate Richards, who decided to put off a move to the "Big Apple" and instead open her dream business right here—in the heart of the Midwest. On the floor above us in our office building is architect Victor Saroki, whose dozen-person firm has helped shape the image and look of southeastern Michigan through his residential and commercial buildings.

Farther along our "Main Street," Faisal Hazime and his family of Lebanese immigrants has brought a bit of the Middle East to the Midwest with their Pita Café. We eat there often. The crushed lentil soup "to go" is great during those long winter evenings when we're working late at our office.

As we see it, that's what business is about. That sense of community, the connections between people, and the pursuit of the dream to run your own show. Whether you want to change your own world or change the world at large, running your own business is an extraordinary way to do it.

And the message is going global. In Africa, people are learning the power of entrepreneurship through the impact of individuals like Mike Korchinsky. His business, Wildlife Works, was launched in a Kenyan village to provide villagers work making wildlife-themed T-shirts instead of engaging in poaching and prostitution. In the Middle East, Israel's economy has become synonymous with high-tech startups. In Asia, Chinese entrepreneurship is giving rise to a middle class that has the power to buy goods and services from around the world. And the new Russia is being shaped by eager entrepreneurs who have embraced capitalism with wild abandon.

As for why we Sloan brothers are so passionate about entrepreneurship, a quick overview of our background gives you a sense. We began back when we were ages 27 (Jeff) and 20 (Rich) with the invention and commercialization of the Battery Buddy, a device to prevent dead batteries in cars. Before that, we worked together on several of Jeff's ventures, including managing rock bands, renovating H.U.D. houses, and breeding and selling Arabian horses. Since 1988, whether through starting up our own businesses, investing, coaching, partnering, or the like, we've helped numerous entrepreneurs realize their ambitions to own their own businesses. We secured more than $70 million of investment into these various companies from high-net-worth "angel" investors and venture capitalists. We converted breakthrough technologies into blockbuster businesses. We served on the boards of these young companies to help them grow and prosper.

We love what entrepreneurship has meant for us and are passionate about helping others realize their dreams of business ownership as well.

Throughout all those years and all those ventures, we've had our fair share of failures but have had enough success to achieve most of our goals and live the life we always dreamed of. We've learned a lot along the way about how to start and grow a business—what works and what doesn't. We know many of the realities and pitfalls entrepreneurs face, from eating a steady diet of peanut-butter-and-jelly sandwiches during those tough startup years to narrowly escaping from venture-capital deals wrought with heavy-handed investment terms that threatened to derail our company.

We know the cold, hard facts about the daunting startup success rates. Out of the millions of Americans who dream about owning their own business, only a fraction will ever do anything more than that—dream. Of those who do take the plunge, many will fail to make it past the first couple of years in business.

But we're proof positive that success is within your reach. We're a couple of ambitious entrepreneurs willing to work hard just like you. We aren't dot-com billionaires. We didn't retire to the Bahamas on our first invention. We still scribble down "to-do lists" at 4 A.M., conjure up new ideas, and then start down that exhilarating path to see if they can be crafted into viable businesses.

Along the way, we've gotten smarter about how to transform those ideas into a successful enterprise. Now we've put all of that wisdom, plus our favorite success stories—and tales of some tough moments—into the pages of this book. By highlighting the issues you'll face, by giving you the smarts you'll need, and by inspiring you to start now, we'll help you move quickly from just dreaming about your idea to starting up and running a business that'll help you lead the life you've always wanted.

We should warn you before you turn this page. Starting up a business is tough work, filled with long hours, big challenges, and sleepless nights. But the rewards are incomparable. The people you'll learn about in this book will prove this. So whatever you do, don't stop dreaming. You're going to need those dreams. But now it's time to start doing. Only *you* have the power to turn your dreams into reality.

It's time to let go of your fears and excuses. It's time to ditch that "I can't do this" attitude. It's time to embark on your journey toward business ownership and the thrilling life of an entrepreneur.

So, *let's start it up!*

CHAPTER ONE

Now Is Always the Best Time to Start Up

Why Now?

We're brothers, best friends, neighbors, and lifelong business partners. We began working together on the Battery Buddy, an invention of ours that prevents dead batteries on cars and boats, in 1987. Remember that year? Specifically, October 19 of that year? They called it "Black Monday," the day the Dow Jones Industrial Average fell 22.6 percent, the largest one-day decline in the market's history.

For the next six years, America's economy was in shock.

But we persevered and cobbled together a successful business. In 1990, we nailed a lucrative licensing deal for the Battery Buddy with a multibillion-dollar industrial colossus named Masco Industries.

In the early 1990s, when the economy was still weak, we leveraged our success as inventors and built a business around helping other inventors license their inventions to big corporations. In exchange, we would receive a portion of any future royalties generated from the licensing deals. Building on that success, we've gone on to develop a portfolio of companies over a 10-year run, along with a venture capital fund to seed new ventures. Ultimately, this path led us to the launch of StartupNation, our current company—and our total passion.

Through it all, we weathered some scary years—two stock market crashes, two wars, terrorist attacks, the implosion of the "New Economy," not to mention the multitude of challenges that we faced inherent in starting and growing our own entrepreneurial endeavors. But we worked our way through the obstacle course with a combination of resilience, tenacity, and a sheer love of what we were doing. In fact, we managed to flourish.

Perhaps you have your own business idea but you can't quite seem to get started. Maybe you're still suffering from a New Economy hangover or just the fear and confusion that's so common if you've never "gone for it" before. Perhaps you think you should wait just a little longer before making the leap to pursue your own dream business.

We beg to differ. Something we believe emphatically is:

Now Is *Always* the Best Time to Start Your Business

That's right. Right now. We truly believe that it's possible for your business to succeed no matter what the economy is doing, no matter what stock market sectors are up or down, or what niches venture capitalists think are hot or not. Many of our country's most successful companies were born during the toughest of times.

We believe that many of the reasons businesses fail have far more to do with factors you *can* control than the ones you *cannot* control. Certainly, unexpected events, such as the terrorist attacks of September 11, 2001, can serve up a situation that could be impossible to overcome for a business—big or small. You can't control world affairs. You can't control the economy. You certainly can't control the stock market, and you're *never* going to control venture capitalists. But in general, events and issues outside your control do not have to ruin your chances for success as an entrepreneur.

You *can* control how much research you do on your big idea. You *can* control which strategies you choose to include in your business plan and how you spend your money. You *can* control whom you hire, and you certainly have control over charting your business's course for the future.

---

5 REASONS TO START A BUSINESS NOW

1. Technology levels the playing field between you and big business.
2. Today, the phrase "corporate job security" is an oxymoron.
3. The Internet provides an unprecedented opportunity to start an online business at minimal cost.
4. Like never before, business can be done from home.
5. Corporate outsourcing to smaller businesses creates an abundance of opportunities.

Bonus Reason: The only person who can boss you around is *you!*

Where do we get this somewhat crazy idea that no matter what the rest of the world is doing, *now* is always the best time to start your own business? From our in-the-trenches experiences riding out two major gyrations in the economy in the past 16 years. From our exposure to thousands of other successful entrepreneurs in our StartupNation community. And as hosts of a live syndicated radio show where we interact with entrepreneurs nationally. We know of thousands of businesses that have hung the "Open for Business" sign on their doors just before and just after the dot-com bust. Many of them have succeeded beyond their wildest imaginations. Indeed, for many, believing that "*now* is always the best time to start your new business" has put them in a far better position for success than if they'd waited for the economy to turn around.

Now, we know it's all too easy to push back, to stick with whatever you've believed up until this moment—whatever has kept you from starting up. We deal with those roadblocks from quagmired callers all the time on our radio show. What we've found is that people hesitate for one of two reasons—either they're immobilized by fear of what they don't know, or they're scared away by what they think they *do* know. Myths about starting up a business are rampant, leading people to use those myths as the crutch that keeps them from moving forward.

So, the first thing we have to do is start busting apart those myths.

Startups—Debunking the Myths

M Y T H   # 1 :   **"Four out of five businesses fail within five years."**

T R U T H   # 1 :   **The fact is, research shows that 40 percent of businesses actually succeed beyond the five year mark.**

For as long as we can remember, conventional wisdom has held that more than 80 percent of businesses—four out of five—fail in their first five years of operation.

Bruce Kirchoff, a former chief economist with the Small Business Administration and now a professor of business at the New Jersey Institute of Technology, confirmed for us that nothing could be further from the truth. The "four out of five" statistic has bedeviled him ever since his boss asked him to find out whether the statistic "four out of five businesses fail" was accurate enough to use in a speech. His first brush with the data revealed that there was no sound research to support the statistic.

Bruce was intrigued. If that number wasn't right, then what was the failure rate? By culling through millions of pieces of data about business success and failure, he was able to come up with what he believes is a more accurate reflection of reality. Forty percent of the businesses he researched were still thriving and succeeding *six years* after startup. Only 18 percent of the companies he researched actually filed for bankruptcy during that period.

As Bruce combed through millions of records of small businesses, he realized much of the data was incomplete. Records didn't show if someone had simply retired. The records didn't do a good job of keeping track of businesses that changed their names or the way they were incorporated. The data certainly didn't follow companies that shut down and then opened in a different location. Erroneously all of those circumstances had been incorrectly lumped into the "failure" category, when in fact they really just encompassed events that were part of doing business. As Bruce found, those stats are extremely misleading.

It's true that businesses do fail, and at a higher rate than any of us would like. Hector Barreto, current administrator of the Small Business Administration, shared with us his view on how to reduce that failure rate significantly. "We've found that if small-business owners do their homework, use the right technology, and heed advice about how to run their business, their chances for success go up exponentially." We couldn't agree more!

MYTH #2: "The dot-com bust proved that technology is not all it was hyped up to be."

TRUTH #2: While many of the dot-com companies went bust due to bad business fundamentals, the technology spawned in the late 1990s is here to stay.

Technology is having a profoundly positive impact on the way business is done. In fact, it's the *game changer*—the single most significant enabler for startups today. We can't think of a time when so many great technologies at ever-decreasing prices have been available to such a huge swath of society. More significantly, many of these technologies—complex software programs, wireless communications, and the Internet, to name just a few—are making it possible for small businesses to act "big" while maintaining the flexibility and innovative qualities inherent in being small.

Here's a quick look at how three technologies are already helping small businesses "act big."

- **Software:** A decade ago, software programs that managed inventories, payrolls, or customer contacts were out of reach for many of the smaller businesses. The companies that offered great customer-management or inventory-control programs—IBM, Oracle, and Siebel—required multimillion-dollar contracts that only major corporations with thousands of employees could justify. But today, even the 16 million home-based entrepreneurs can easily access such software systems by purchasing "off-the-shelf" versions like QuickBooks or through web-based products from companies like Netsuite.com.

- **Wireless:** There's no doubt that wireless technology is making it far easier to be a business owner, increasing the flexibility and freedom that have long been the hallmarks of being an entrepreneur. Today, with wireless technology, you can be on a sales call while monitoring your inventory levels on your wireless personal digital assistant. With a wireless connection for your computer, you can take a meeting at your local Starbucks while staying on top of the orders coming into your website in real time. And you can take one more important call on your cell phone before the door on the airplane closes. The thing about wireless technology is that it allows you to always be "plugged in" to your business for maximum efficiency.

- **Internet:** Want a worldwide market? Want to do exhaustive research? How about low-cost marketing and advertising? Or how about creating a storefront viewable by people *well beyond* your Main Street? Through the Internet you can do all of this—from business logistics, to customer communications, to selling what you offer—and it's all possible without ever leaving your home office.

DIAMONDS CAN BE AN ENTREPRENEUR'S BEST FRIEND: BLUENILE.COM

The best way we can describe just how powerful all of this technology is for your business is to tell you about one of the great Internet success stories: BlueNile.com.

The online jewelry store's founder, Mark Vadon, is one of our favorite examples of a smart, tough entrepreneur who used the Internet to his best advantage, even when many people thought he was going to crash and burn like so many other dot-coms.

As Mark told us in 2003, he was able to harness all the upside of the Internet to create a jewelry powerhouse that could compete against deep-pocketed brick-and-mortar companies such as Zales.

Putting the Internet to work, Blue Nile managed to take on the traditional brick-and-mortar competition, selling well north of $100 million in jewelry in 2004 with just 115 full-time employees and a 10,000-square-foot warehouse. If Blue Nile were a traditional jewelry retailer, it would need about 150 stores and 1,000 employees to do that same level of business. All those stores and employees force jewelers to take a markup of 60 to 70 percent to make profitable margins. By keeping

(continued on next page)

overhead at a minimum, Mark can keep prices low and provide more value to customers.

But as Mark told us, the Internet isn't just about cheap prices. "Cheap prices would get people to surf our site, but that doesn't necessarily mean they're going to buy," he says. Most jewelry buyers are used to trying on jewelry and having a salesperson nearby to answer questions about size, carats, and quality. Mark knew he had to overcome those two big sticking points. He did it in a simple but smart way. As he built his company, he remained focused on the idea of filling Blue Nile's website with information he thought his customers would find relevant, like honest, factual information about a diamond's characteristics. Today he offers comprehensive online tutorials about how to select the best ring. Just in case that didn't do the trick, BlueNile.com offers a 30-day, money-back guarantee if the person receiving the jewelry isn't satisfied.

Mark's experience using technology to build Blue Nile's success is living proof of how powerful technology can be for a small business.

INTERNET STATISTICS

Here's a look at just how vast and diverse the Internet audience is today (2004 statistics):

- Worldwide Internet usage reached 813 million people
- Nearly 75 percent or 204.3 million Americans have access to the Internet from home
- 50 percent of Americans with a household income under $50,000 shop the Internet
- 59 percent of African Americans shop online
- 63 percent of Hispanics shop online. Hispanics are the fastest-growing online population and are younger than the Internet population in general.
- 49 percent of senior citizens shop online
- Total online sales in the U.S.: $101 billion

- 75 percent of small businesses have an online presence
- The average male spends more money shopping online per month than the average female—$204 to $186, respectively.

Sources: Nielsen/NetRatings, 2004, Yahoo! Harris Interactive 2004, Shop.org 2004

M Y T H   # 3 : **"All the money guys are still spooked because of the dot-com bust."**

T R U T H   # 3 : **The money guys are *always* spooked! The explosion of capital in the late 1990s was an aberration, not a reality. That doesn't mean you can't get money for your startup; you just have to present a business opportunity based on solid fundamentals.**

Let's face it—it's never been easy to score capital for entrepreneurial ventures. But for a brief, intoxicating moment during the dot-com boom, money was easy to come by, especially for any business that had the moniker "dot-com" as part of its name. We now know that the dot-com era was an ill-conceived fantasy, not reality. In reality, the money guys are always tough to persuade.

They should be.

If someone's going to invest money in your business, they deserve to have a well-thought-out business plan with a strong focus on how you're going to reach profitability and create an enticing return on investment. This is what drives rational investing decisions.

We're happy to see this return to more rational approaches to funding businesses. We think when investors and lenders make the bar higher and harder to leap over, new companies are more likely to really think through their business and financing strategies. We believe that makes for far stronger companies and ups the likelihood of success in the long run.

Don't misunderstand—we do believe that capital is readily available for your startup. You just need to know where to look and how to position yourself. We'll give you a lot more detail in Chapter Six on how to find money, and how much and what kind of money are best for you and your startup.

FAST FACTS: MONEY

- Most single-person businesses start up with an average of $6,000 in capital.
- In 2004, the Small Business Administration raised its small-business loan caps from $750,000 to $2 million. Approximately $50 million in loan guaranties were provided each day.
- In 2003, angel investors (high-net-worth private investors) provided over $18 billion to startup and early-stage companies. This dwarfs the amount venture capitalists (professional investors who manage investment funds) provide to startups in a typical year.

FINANCING IN A BAD YEAR: ATHLETA

Those concerned about securing financing can take heart in the story of Scott Kerslake, the founder of the women's sports apparel company called Athleta. If Scott had listened to the myth that "the money guys are spooked," his Petaluma, California, catalog and website business would never have grown to $30 million in sales by 2004.

Scott went shopping for venture capital in one of the worst years ever, 2002. He needed money to expand his warehouse and invest in technology that would allow customers to find out immediately if those "must-have" running shorts were in or out of stock.

"The venture capital market was very challenging and the standards a company had to meet to receive funding were extraordinarily high," said

Scott. But he was determined to raise the money so Athleta could capture a bigger slice of the $38 billion women's athletic apparel market.

Scott had started up in 1997, at the cusp of the dot-com bubble. It was an era when startups were shaping themselves to be anything and everything they thought investors wanted to hear, but Athleta built a business plan based on good old-fashioned business fundamentals, and set goals that focused on long-term success. Rather than take on a large investment initially, the company requested just enough money to meet well-defined milestones. Scott also assembled a very talented management team. Lastly, he created a brand that clearly resonated with women, the niche he was targeting within the sports apparel industry. It was these assets and Scott's conservative approach that appealed to investors in 2002.

The outcome? Scott secured $6 million in financing when most people couldn't even get a meeting with a venture capitalist.

MYTH #4: **"I shouldn't quit my job and leave behind a 'sure thing' paycheck, benefits, and health care to pursue a dream business of my own!"**

TRUTH #4: **Corporate job security is at an all-time low. With the growing trend of "offshoring" jobs and productivity soaring, many jobs are simply disappearing.**

Once upon a time, it was easy to find people who worked for one company for decades. Perhaps you knew such a person—a friend or maybe even your mother or father. But today, many have a different story. Dot-com carnage aside, it might be somebody who's been "reengineered" out of a once-secure corporate job. Maybe it's somebody whose business function has been outsourced to a sub-minimum-wage but highly skilled laborer in another country. In the tech industry alone—usually a bastion of well-paying American jobs—over 100,000 jobs have gone overseas since 2000.

Perhaps it's somebody who's been replaced by technology that has helped America's productivity soar 14 percent since 2001.

FAST FACTS: ASPIRING ENTREPRENEURS

In a 2004 survey conducted by Federal Express, 67 percent of those polled said they dream of owning their own business. Fifty-five percent indicated that they would leave their current job to start their own business if resources were not an issue.

We know it's tough to leave behind the so-called security blanket of a corporate job to start up a business that may take years to become profitable or even worse, may fail altogether. But as the economy softened in the early 2000s, so did the notion of corporate job security. Since then, salaries have stagnated. More important, many jobs have simply disappeared. That's especially true among the ranks of white-collar workers who believed their jobs were a lot more secure than those of their blue-collar brethren.

Corporate America has quickly learned that a cubicle can be replicated overseas just as easily as a shop floor can.* Corporate America has also learned that the workers in those cubicles can be replaced by a new piece of technology that does their job faster and more efficiently.

Indeed, white-collar jobs are experiencing the same phenomenon that hit blue-collar manufacturing jobs in the 1980s.

Here are a few statistics that show just how vulnerable the once-hallowed corporate job really is. From 2001 to 2004, the United States lost 2.7 million jobs, with 300,000 going overseas and the rest disappearing due to gains in productivity.† Indeed, it appears the real ogre behind the job losses is the rapid increase in

---

Fortune magazine, June 23, 2003, "Down and Out in White Collar America."
†Study by research firm Forrester Research Inc., reported in *Business Week*'s special report "Where Are the Jobs?" March 22, 2004.

productivity over the past several years. For every percentage-point gain in productivity, we lose 1.3 million jobs. With productivity growing at an annual rate of more than 3 percent even during the recession, jobs that once seemed secure have been whacked away.

White-collar jobs aren't the only ones at risk. In fact, jobs that once seemed critical and important because you needed a "human" to do them are also being lost. For instance, retailing had always been an employee-intensive business. You needed clerks at the cash register to ring up your consumers' purchases. Not anymore. Most of us have probably used one of those self-checkout counters at Home Depot or your local grocery store. Travel to Europe, as we do frequently, and you'll see automated convenience stores where there's not a single person in sight. Everything is sold through vending machines! And coming soon at Schippol Airport in Amsterdam, you will board your plane without ever interacting with a gate agent. Boarding passes will soon be taken by a virtual gate agent—a scanner—that will confirm your identity and allow you onboard.

More important, as your own boss, you'll never have to fear that someone will walk into your office—or cubicle—at any minute and unexpectedly hand you your walking papers. When you call the shots, there's no chance you'll be blindsided by a pink slip. You'll have perspective on how the business is performing and adjust plans and resources accordingly. This will give you the ability to manage your future instead of some "superior" in the corporate ranks who is only after making sure his or her department meets its bottom line.

We're certainly not alone in believing that creating your own business can be a more secure option for you. Even the universities and colleges that once readied students for the corporate world are getting into the entrepreneurial act.

The National Commission on Entrepreneurship says that now more than 550 colleges and universities offer classes in entrepreneurship, with 49 of them offering degree programs. "People realize that rather than get a job, I've got to make a job," Erik Pages, policy director for the commission, told the Associated Press in 2003.

MYTH #5: "The big companies always squash the small companies in the end. Just look at Wal-Mart!"

TRUTH #5: Small business can beat big business—you just have to play to the inherent strengths of small business. And remember—Wal-Mart was once a small business!

It's true that small businesses are being challenged more and more by the big guys. As an example, overbearing "Big Box" retailers use their immense buying power to price their products lower than most small businesses are able to. But before you start thinking that the "big guys" will always beat you with lower pricing, think again. There's a proven way you can compete and win. It's all about building relationships and providing better customer service. The big-box retailers' business model can't afford to implement the kind of customer service that you can. And the power of strong relationships can be extremely persuasive when consumers make their spending decisions.

Mike Palmer and his store, Premier Pet Supply, in Beverly Hills, Michigan, proves the point. His single-location, family-owned pet store opened its doors in 1992 and is thriving despite the ever-growing presence of "Big Box" pet-supply retailers. Today, there are 14 of them—Petco, Petsmart, and others—within a 30-mile radius! Mike's edge is all about the relationships he establishes with his customers and the superior service he provides them. "I train my salespeople in two powerful ways. First, I want them to be courteous, personable, and attentive. Second, I require that they be educated about pets, about the products we offer, and about our customers' specific needs," Mike says. "In some cases, we're better off telling a customer not to buy a particular product, because it may not be necessary," and though his company may lose a sale on that particular product, he'll create a repeat customer that appreciates the honesty, has confidence in his advice, and buys more over time. "Our customers become customers for life," he says.

Due to the strength of the relationships he's built with customers, Mike has even been able to discontinue expensive advertising and rely instead on word of mouth. He makes a point of getting out in the community and sponsoring local neighborhood activities, like kids' pet shows. The result: Mike's profits have gone up year over year since he opened.

How do we know Mike's story so well? Because we shop there. Yes, we may pay a little more for his products, but we get the right stuff and always like saying hello to Mike as we pass through his store looking for the latest, greatest dog treats.

For another example, just read about Lavetta Willis's company, Dada Footwear.

GOING TOE TO TOE WITH THE BIG GUYS: DADA FOOTWEAR

When Lavetta Willis founded the hip street-fashion brand Dada, she proved that being big wasn't the key factor in persuading the likes of NBA legend Karl Malone to wear *her* shoes instead of shoes from the "big guys."

Lavetta talked to us in 2003 on StartupNation Radio about how she competed effectively against much larger brands like Nike and Reebok. Here's what she had to say:

First, I didn't start out with basketball shoes. I started out trying to simply reach the urban market. I made Dada-branded hats and began selling them out of the trunk of my car in New York City and Washington, D.C. I'd sell them at any street scene I could find. Anything to reach consumers.

(continued on next page)

I decided on hats first, because they're relatively easy to make. You can buy a lot of hats, stamp your brand on them, and start selling them right away. And back then I didn't know anything about how to manufacture shoes.

But once I started getting buzz about my hats and my brand, I decided it was time to branch out to shoes. Once I had some prototypes and was ready to sell, I sat in the lobby of Foot Locker's corporate headquarters while the rest of my team was out on the street selling hats. I knew I needed to team up with a big distributor. But I also knew they needed to see why they should carry Dada. I knew they needed to hear about Dada from the buzz on the street, not just from me. Those efforts paid off big time for us. Foot Locker signed on to distribute our shoes. Then we started going after some basketball stars.

Enter her deal with Karl Malone and a host of other major basketball stars. Sales rocketed as fans began to notice what those stars were wearing up and down the court—Dada shoes.

Lavetta told us she started out thinking a lot about how she was going to compete with the big guys. "But I ended up thinking more about how to make a shoe perform great and look cool," she said. "It's absolutely necessary to separate your products and your marketing from the bigger competition."

MYTH #6: "I should wait for the economy to improve before starting my business."

TRUTH #6: If you're waiting for the economy to improve, you might miss out on a great opportunity for your business. If you start now, you'll be in prime position when the economy does improve.

When we were getting started with developing our invention, the Battery Buddy, we knew it was impossible to control or predict what the economy was going to do. So instead we focused on what we *could* control and predict. We continued to research the

Battery Buddy's effectiveness, worked with engineers to perfect the prototype, and never gave up on the belief that our invention was important and unique enough to be commercialized.

By staying the course through the downswing in the economy in the late 1980s, we were perfectly positioned to take advantage of the upswing in the economy that came in the mid-1990s. When it did, we were right where we wanted to be. We had commercialized one great invention and were more than ready to leverage our track record and street smarts to help other inventors take their ideas to market.

The "Green" Limo: Evo

The story of Seth Seaberg and David Young is one of our favorite stories about why it's so important not to put your dreams on hold just because the economy is hurting. You never know when the market is going to surprise you and make your product a huge hit.

It was just after the NASDAQ hit bottom in 2001 when Seth and David decided to quit their jobs in advertising and in artist management to start up a limousine service based in Los Angeles.

Now, granted, Los Angeles probably didn't need another limo service. But the two young entrepreneurs had a great idea that they knew would set them apart from the crowd: environmentally friendly limos in the form of big black sport-utility vehicles. The two of them used their own savings to convert GMC Yukons and Chevy Suburbans from gas-guzzlers to sippers of compressed natural gas, a cleaner, cheaper fuel than regular unleaded.

They dubbed their company Evo.

Hollywood loved it. Some of the city's biggest stars who shared a concern for the environment, including Woody Harrelson and Cameron Diaz, picked Evo to ferry them around L.A. In just two years, the two had built their limo business into a great brand with solid cash flow. They added little in-car perks, like a minibar service that featured organic soy vodka and good-for-you snacks like organic trail mix. They

(continued on next page)

hired informed drivers who could talk about how the sport-utility vehicles were converted to compressed natural gas, and just what the environmental benefits were.

Evo's limos were in high demand not only because they were "cool" but because they were environmentally friendly at the same time. Then came Evo's big break. Gas prices skyrocketed in California in 2004, topping out at more than $3 a gallon. They actually started getting calls from customers asking about converting their private cars to natural gas. It was a business they'd always wanted to be in, and the expertise they had amassed, combined with the gas crisis of 2004, had them sitting pretty.

"If we'd waited for the economy to turn around before launching our natural-gas-powered limo service, Dave and I would've missed a golden opportunity to pursue a huge opportunity in converting people's cars to natural gas at the moment when the market wanted it most," Seth told us.

By 2004, Evo was ramping up to do the first of its "custom conversions," starting with Kevin Richardson of the Backstreet Boys. Kevin had Evo convert his gas-guzzling GMC Yukon into a mean, *green* machine. He even had Evo install a home-refueling station in his garage so he can fill up from the same lines that heat his home.

Evo's success throughout the tough economic times also meant that they were first in line for an infusion of capital when venture capitalists caught wind of their story. They were able to raise enough capital to make plans, as of this writing, to expand their limo fleet from three to 12 by early 2005. They've also set their sights on expanding to San Francisco and New York.

CHAPTER TWO

How We Started Up and What We Learned Along the Way

Our Paths Converge

It was 1987. We'd been living thousands of miles apart for years. Rich was a freshman at the University of Colorado in Boulder, majoring in Asian history. Jeff was in his mid-twenties, living in Birmingham, Michigan, about an hour's drive from Flint, where we grew up and where our parents still lived. That's when Jeff had an idea for an invention.

Jeff: My Entrepreneurial Epiphany

I was sitting in my car outside a restaurant near Flint, listening to the Giants wallop the Broncos in Super Bowl XXI before I headed home.

I watched a young guy exit the restaurant and jump in his car to leave. He turned the key. Nothing. Turned it again. Nothing. He'd left his lights on while he grabbed dinner, like a lot of us have done. He got out of his car in the cold rain to ask people for jumper cables. I felt bad for the guy. I didn't have a set. In fact, nobody in the parking lot did. He ended up calling a tow truck to get a jump.

As the tow truck pulled in, I had this epiphany. The poor

guy's dead battery represented a huge opportunity. There's noth-
ing worse than walking out to find your car deader than a door-
nail, especially on a dark, rainy night in winter. If I could figure
out how to stop batteries from going dead when the lights were
left on, I'd have a great invention that I could sell to consumers.

There was just one big problem with me being the one to
solve the problem of dead batteries—I didn't know the first
thing about how car batteries worked.

We'd always planned to work together—we just weren't sure
how or when it would happen. We began a series of long distance
conversations about the possibility of joining forces to bring Jeff's
battery saver "idea" to market. After numerous hours on the
phone, we convinced ourselves that this was the opportunity we'd
been looking for. We were ready to embark on a new business
together—commercializing the invention that Jeff had brainstormed that night at the restaurant. It would eventually become
known as the Battery Buddy, so named by Julie, our marketing-
minded sister. In concept, the Battery Buddy would protect you
from a dead battery by preventing excessive battery drain if you
accidentally left your car lights on.

Part of the Battery Buddy's appeal was the likelihood that it
was patentable. Getting a patent was a big deal for us. Years
before, our mom had told us at the dinner table one night, "If you
boys really want to do something, to leave a mark, a legacy, you
should get a patent on an invention of your own." She would
read aloud the patents featured in the Monday *New York Times*,
fascinating us with inventors' accomplishments.

Rich: The Train Ride Home to Flint

Watching the countryside pass by, I thought about how long I'd
lived away from the family. First it was boarding school starting

at age 14, and then on to college in Colorado. What if Jeff and I couldn't work together after all that time apart? Worse, what if I hated being in "business"? I'd had one brush with the corporate world, making cold calls for a leading investment firm in New York the summer before. It was a nightmare—it just wasn't for me. All I could think of was that office, filled with guys in white shirts with blue suits and ties. Was I heading to that world of conformity and conventionality?

I knew that that kind of life would mean certain death for my free-spirited creative nature. I was thinking, What if working with Jeff on this invention turned out to be that kind of "business"?

When we met on the train station platform, our worries faded, taking a back seat to the thrilling thought that we were about to start living our dream. By the time we'd piled all of the college duffel bags into Jeff's hand-me-down Jeep, we were talking about the Battery Buddy nonstop. We talked about Jeff's first attempt for a patent on the device. The application had been rejected. What were the next steps? How would we divide the work? What did we need to do for the new patent application? Where were we going to find engineers to make a prototype for us? By the time we arrived home at our parents' house for a reunion dinner, we were filled with passion, energy, and excitement for our "big idea."

Little did we know as we finished dessert and caught up with our parents and sister, Julie, that we'd need every bit of that energy and excitement to make the Battery Buddy a success.

In the months that followed, we had many ups and downs. A definite downer was when a licensing deal we had high hopes for with a major manufacturer-distributor completely fell through at the eleventh hour. But on the positive side, we were heartened by the headway we were making together. Though we were still waiting for a response from the U.S. Patent and Trademark Office about our second patent application, we had word from Masco Industries that they were toying with the idea of licensing our product from us. Masco Industries was a big deal in the Detroit automotive industry. At that time, the company earned $88 on every single car made in America by supplying auto parts to companies such as Ford Motor Co. and General Motors Corp.

What we loved about Masco Industries was its entrepreneurial roots. Alex Manoogian started the parent company in 1929 based on innovative ideas like the single-handle washerless faucet he perfected and then manufactured for Delta's faucet business. For us, Masco's love of new ideas felt like a good fit.

But Masco Industries, now a New York Stock Exchange juggernaut, wasn't going to automatically leap at the chance to license the Battery Buddy and make the Sloan brothers rich. We needed to convince them that we were for real and that the Battery Buddy was a marketable product. In finding ways to do that, we went on a crash course in business basics, reading as much as we could and talking to whoever we thought was smart. We were novices with one old typewriter and a case of Wite-Out. We'd splurged on just one thing: fancy letterhead and business cards that proclaimed us as "Sloan Products, Inc., a division of Sloan Corporation." On the face of it, our letterhead had us appearing as legit as Masco.

With some of Jeff's savings and small loans from Mom and Dad, we were able to get through those days when there was virtually no money coming in the door. We'd perfected the art of making peanut-butter-and-jelly sandwiches and showing up "coincidentally" just as Mom was putting food on the table at home. We use that experience to this day as a way to explain to others how to keep expenses low when you're starting out—we call it the "PB&J Budget."

Our limited finances, however, weren't the toughest part of making a go of this new venture. We were totally inexperienced in commercializing an invention. Neither one of us had ever taken a class on business or engineering.

Never afraid to ask for help, we set up meetings with the brightest minds in the automotive business. Our first—and what ended up being one of our most important meetings—was with David Cole, PhD, the highly respected director of the Center for Automotive Research at the University of Michigan. David knew everybody who was anybody in the automotive industry. When we told him we were looking for a great engineer to help us make a marketable version of the Battery Buddy, he responded immediately, "I know the guy. John Auman." He told us about how John had been a manager at the General Motors Tech Center, responsible for managing the development of advanced technologies.

When we met John, the chemistry between us was instant. For much of 1989, John worked with us very closely to create a working Battery Buddy prototype. Throughout that year, we would come to depend heavily on John's knowledge and expertise.

His biggest contribution to our business careers was teaching us the value of what he called "project management." Each week, we'd get together with John over coffee in the living room of his home to review our progress relative to the development plan John had created at the outset of the project. This discipline kept us organized and on schedule—wisdom that we've put into practice ever since.

John, however, did more than help us with the development of the Battery Buddy prototype—he believed in us *personally*. We were just two young guys from Flint with no engineering and almost no business background to speak of. Having this 30-year engineering veteran put his faith in us and our idea was a huge validation of our efforts. He became one of our earliest mentors. To this day, a framed photo of John hangs on the wall in our boardroom, reminding us of his guidance and inspiration.

In late 1989, we snagged a meeting with Masco Industries to make our pitch to license the Battery Buddy to them. We drove to their headquarters confident in our product and its potential. We were escorted to an impressive boardroom. The doors closed behind us, and we were in session. We demonstrated a crude yet functional prototype of the Battery Buddy that we had created with John's guidance. It worked beautifully.

While neither one of us can remember taking a full breath during that meeting, we felt it was going really well. That is, until one of the Masco engineers in the meeting spoke up. "Look, I can see that the product works, but this thing looks pretty bulky. Will it fit under the hood of a car?" Admittedly, the working prototype was much larger than the finished product would be, but we thought everyone in the room would understand that our prototype was intended solely to prove the invention worked, not how it would appear or be installed. We'd assumed that they'd be able to imagine that the finished product would be far sleeker and more compact, designed to be compatible with virtually any car.

We could feel the mood shift in the room from totally positive to really reluctant. As a typical large corporation, it would be easier and safer for them to say "NO." We were too close to succeeding to let that happen. Jeff said, "Then we'll make another prototype that will look exactly like the finished product." Rich finished Jeff's thought: "And we'll prove it fits. We'll be back in two days."

That night we found ourselves on the campus of University of Michigan, where Rich had transferred. We went into the student woodshop and crafted an exact-scale nonfunctioning prototype. By midnight, Rich had painted it and put the final touches on our logo to make the piece look more professional. The next morning, we drove to every car dealership in Ann Arbor, domestic and foreign. At each, we asked to look under the hood of cars on display. We attached the wooden Battery Buddy prototype next to the battery where it would be installed in the real-world application and took a photo showing the perfect fit.

We "installed" the prototype on 80 car and truck models that day. We dropped the film off just as the one-hour photo shop closed. The next morning, we spun by the photo shop, picked up our developed pictures, and compiled a bursting three-ring binder filled with our analysis and documentation. By 4 P.M. that day, we were standing in front of the executive assistant's desk at Masco Industries. We asked to see Louis Merz, the VP who had the ultimate power to decide the fate of the Battery Buddy. We handed him the heavy binder. He started leafing through, slowly at first; after a while, he just kept flipping the pages, a slight smile on his face. "Okay, guys, we're back on track. Let's keep going with this."

We had turned a "NO" into a "maybe." But before we walked out of his office, Lou assigned us one last task. He wanted us to take the next few weeks to build one more prototype—a functioning Battery Buddy in its true and final form.

We had no choice but to accept the challenge. Between us, though, we knew this would be difficult. In our years working together, we'd learned that unexpected roadblocks were the norm—not the exception—when it comes to designing and engineering brand-new products. And the Battery Buddy was no simple invention. It was an extremely complex electro-mechanical device that had to survive under a car's hood—a hellish environment for any product. We wondered what roadblock would confront us in the days ahead.

We would find out soon enough. The problem came a few weeks later in the form of a broken prototype part. It was the night before our final meeting and would result in a midnight drive across the state and back.

The Midnight Ride

It was the spring of 1990. Believe it or not, our efforts to land a licensing deal with Masco Industries were *still* inconclusive.

We looked at the clock on the dashboard of our Jeep. It was

1:15 A.M., Monday morning, and we were totally exhausted. We had 200 miles left to drive and a make-or-break presentation to nail at Masco Industries' headquarters the next morning. Just maybe, *finally*, we would ink a deal with them that would take the Battery Buddy from sketchpad to commercial success. We were jittery from too many cups of coffee, and more than a little panicked that we'd never make it back to our home office in time to take showers, put on our suits, and get to a meeting that could change our lives forever.

We knew all too well what the other was thinking as we pulled into a deserted rest stop just outside of Grand Rapids, Michigan, to switch drivers. As twenty-something brothers who'd spent years working together and dreaming our business into reality, we could read each other's minds.

"What are we doing on the road in the middle of the night hunting down engineering parts? Was this long drive, accompanied by bad coffee and static on the radio, really what we had dreamed about when we made a pact to run our own business?"

The night's drama had started six hours earlier in our small apartment, a location known to our business contacts as "Sloan Corporation World Headquarters." We had ordered in pizza as we were putting the finishing touches on our presentation for the meeting with Masco Industries. At this final meeting, we were to present our market research, engineering drawings, production-cost estimates, focus-group study results, and our final prototype—and Masco was to say a conclusive "YES" or "NO." By around 8 P.M., the presentation started coming off the printer that sat on the floor of our "world headquarters" a few feet from the bed. We knew we had to wow the Masco executives.

The assembly of the prototype was complete. But as we tested it one last time, one of the key components broke. Even worse, it was a custom, one-of-a-kind part made specifically for our design.

Without it, the Battery Buddy would not work.

We knew the demo had to be a grand slam or Masco Industries would have every right to turn us down. We *couldn't* let that happen. We'd come too far and risked too much. Immediately, we phoned the engineer who had originally designed and manufactured the component for us and asked him what we should do.

He said, "Well, I've got some good news and I've got some bad news. The good news is I made a duplicate part, the second of which I have with me. The bad news is, *it's here with me*, it's Sunday night, and I'm clear across the state. There's no way I can get it to you in time for your presentation tomorrow morning."

To us, the next move was clear. We looked at each other and said, "Who's driving?"

We dropped everything. Our presentation was strewn across the floor. The copier was still spewing out pages as we jumped into the car and headed for the highway for the eight-hour round-trip drive to pick up the critical part.

We arrived at the engineer's home at midnight in the middle of the boonies, picked up the missing part, turned the car back onto the road, and headed for home.

Rich's Transformation

Rich: I glanced at my brother slumped in the passenger seat trying to get some shut-eye before he had to take the wheel again. During the three years it had taken us to land this final meeting with Masco, he'd always been there to come up with a quick solution to a problem, put in those extra hours of work, pump up our enthusiasm, and get us back on track. We were both driven by this passion to do something on our own, to do it "our way." But Jeff was truly unstoppable. He just never quit believing in the business or in us.

As we sped along the highway, I thought about how we had to do everything possible to make the Battery Buddy a suc-

cess. As I rolled down the window of our Jeep and gulped in fresh air to wake up, I had to admit that being in business as an entrepreneur was as creative and exhilarating as anything I could imagine. I felt alive, bold, committed to something important. Without a doubt I wanted to be in business, and I wanted my brother at my side every step of the way. I put the pedal to the metal. For some reason, I couldn't get the words of the writer Goethe out of my mind: "What you can do, or dream you can do, begin it! Boldness has genius, power, and magic in it." I'd never felt so committed in my life.

At 4 A.M., we finally arrived back at our apartment building and dragged ourselves inside. We had to organize the presentation, complete the prototype, and test it to make sure it worked. By 6 A.M., we'd managed to pull everything together, testing the prototype on the Jeep as the sun rose. We fell into bed for a couple of hours of sleep. At 8 A.M., the alarm went off and we raced into the showers, shot down a few more cups of coffee, and put on our suits and ties.

There was a palpable silence as we drove to the meeting. We'd pulled out all the stops and had literally gone the extra mile to make this presentation perfect. Whether Masco Industries decided to go forward or not, we could always say that we'd given it our best shot. When we arrived, we were ushered into a big boardroom. After a few minutes, the executives filed in. We stood and shook hands.

It was showtime.

We passed out the presentation, showed off our *working* prototype, and answered a few final questions. We'd been there for only a half hour when several of the executives excused themselves to talk privately. We waited, making small talk with the remaining execs, trying to appear at ease. All they needed to do now was take a final vote. And there we sat, in that plush board-room that early-spring morning in 1990. It was the culmination of countless hours of work for the two of us. It was clear that this was the moment that the Battery Buddy's fate—and ours—would be cast.

The executives filed back into the room. The next few minutes were going to make or break us.

Mr. Merz looked around the table at the dozen executives and said, "All right. Raise your hand if you think we should license the Battery Buddy." We weren't breathing. To our total amazement, one by one, all 12 people raised their hands in a show of support. In just 30 seconds, they made the decision on an invention that had taken us years of hard work to make happen.

We had done it. We were really going to make a go of this business and this life, doing it *our own way*. Sure, "Sloan Products, a division of Sloan Corp." had only one product, a messy home office, and the two of us.

But we were in business.

StartupNation Starts Up

Fast-forward to 2000. Sloan Ventures and our network of angel investors had pooled nearly $70 million and funded multiple companies throughout the technology boom of the late 1990s. By March of that year, the NASDAQ had topped 5,000. In accordance with our financing strategy, we were preparing to raise our next round of money for our company from our angel investors, who included some of the Midwest's most successful entrepreneurs. Mark Morris, Jr., DVM, son of the founder of Science Diet dog food, invested with us. Rich Rogel, a health care entrepreneur, was backing our biotech ventures. Fred Erb, who built up one of the Midwest's largest lumber companies from scratch, was getting his first taste of the high-tech world.

Six weeks later, on April 14, the stock market crashed for the second time in our professional lives. When the markets opened on April 15, 2000, the NASDAQ had fallen to just 3,321 points and, as we would later learn, would tumble much farther. Thousands of Internet companies and high-tech startups would go belly-up, including some of our own, as the world reeled from the dot-com bust.

Angel investors and venture capitalists withered or went away completely. In the months after the crash, the surviving businesses were forced to face the necessity of earning *real* money—now, to fund our young companies in the early going, revenues would have to sustain them instead of invested capital. Because our business model was dependent on angel investors, we were in a tough spot. That source of capital had dried up, and we were forced to develop a new business model or go down like so many others.

As we regrouped, we decided to do what we'd done so many times in the past—talk to a mentor. We went to Sam Valenti, a financial luminary who earned his chops as a highly successful manager of the state of Michigan pension fund.

Sitting in his office, surrounded by plasma-screen TVs blaring financial data and financial cable news, we told him about a business concept we were brewing up. Even in those hard times—perhaps especially in those hard times—there was still huge demand for assistance in starting and running a small business. Many people across the country were scrambling for a way to make a living. Companies weren't hiring—they were only firing. More than ever, people were forced to turn to entrepreneurship as the solution. We thought we had something to offer in this space. Instead of focusing on investing, where to be successful we had to turn *away* 99 percent of the people who came to us, we had a plan for a business that would allow us to turn *on* 99 percent of the people who came to us. We would focus on providing the inspiration and information that we'd culled from years of being entrepreneurs and from affiliating with extremely smart and successful angel investors. We even had a name for the new venture.

We called it "StartupNation."

Sam couldn't have been more supportive. He told us he thought it was the biggest opportunity we'd ever brought into his office. But the thing that lingered with us was when, after a brief pause, Sam just looked at us and shook his head. "You guys are tough. I can't believe how the two of you just keep on going. You never let anything stop you."

We hadn't really thought about it, but it was true. During the past decade, we hadn't let anything stop us in our entrepreneurial adventure. We'd fought off competitors who wanted to steal our Battery Buddy idea. We'd weathered rejected patents and business failures. We'd faced cash crunches that took us down to fumes in our checking account and threatened to completely derail us. But we'd also had enough of a taste of sweet success to keep us going and reassure us that we had the "right stuff." We believed we could do something important with StartupNation—we were onto something that could be transformative for our fellow entrepreneurs. If we did it right, we could dispel the myths, flatten the obstacles, and turn people on to a better way of life. In the process, we could create an exciting business opportunity.

Within months we had StartupNation up and running, with a rapidly growing community of like-minded entrepreneurs seeking new heights in business and in life. Through StartupNation, we've advised many thousands of our fellow entrepreneurs on how to start and then build successful companies. On our radio show, we interview the country's most successful entrepreneurs—people who lead companies we call "Super Startups"—to glean their secrets to success. You'll read about some of them—the Super Start-ups highlighted in the pages ahead. In a feature we call "Coach's Corner," we take calls from people around the country who've got burning questions. Those entrepreneurs-in-waiting are as diverse as a young woman looking for information on how to lease retail space to the middle-aged man thinking about leaving his corporate job who needs a few words of encouragement.

A great deal of what we discuss on StartupNation Radio is grounded in the real-world lessons we learned during our years as inventors, company builders, venture capitalists, and business coaches. Drawing upon these experiences, we've built a philoso-phy about business and entrepreneurship that we're now sharing through StartupNation Radio, our website, and this book.

First and foremost, our philosophy about starting and running a business is built on what's been crucial to our success: *passion*. Even as the "seasoned" businesspeople we are today, we still get that same butterfly-in-the-stomach feeling we had as two twenty-somethings pitching the Battery Buddy, hoping for a big break. We still get high on the idea that we can turn a business dream into a reality. We're still driven every day by the process of discov-ery, of coming up with a great idea, figuring out how to get it to market, and then making it a success.

Second, we believe that business is about more than making money. Of course, financial success is important—we've made mil-lions and helped other entrepreneurs strike it rich. But first and foremost, we are entrepreneurs. For us, business is a way of life—a *lifestyle*. We believe running a business helps us be more fulfilled, engaged, and productive members of our society. Neither of us has an MBA from a fancy business school. Instead, we've both learned what we need to know about business by *doing* it.

We've tried our best to use the power of business to change our lives—and the lives of those around us—for the better. The thrill we get from making this contribution reinvents itself as passion for the company, the product, and the people involved. We're not like the "dot-cons" of the last decade who thought businesses were built to flip or the fakers who thought that valuation had nothing to do with values. For us, being entrepreneurs gives us the opportunity to follow principles we've set down in our own Manifesto:

OUR MANIFESTO

- **Work as Freedom:** We think work is about pursuing our dreams, not for the benefit of some nameless, faceless company, but for ourselves. We believe that owning our own business leads to the liberties and freedoms that the forefathers of our country envisioned for us. We're free to choose the kind of business we conduct. We're free to choose the way we spend our time. We're free to choose the people with whom we work. We're free to set our priorities.

- **Work as Family:** We've tried to create a workplace environment where employees feel like they're actually members of a greater family. There's a sense of common purpose, mutual respect, and deep trust. Everyone should feel important and as though they're a meaningful member of the collective effort. It's an environment that empowers people to share in the hard work—and in the benefits.

- **Work as Fulfillment:** We've made it a priority to ensure that our work gives us a sense of satisfaction. When we wake up in the morning, we can't wait to get on the phone, get online, and get our team in gear. The work we do is truly the work we love. For us there's nothing that turns us on more than facing a challenge and transforming it into an opportunity. There's nothing more thrilling than seeing a customer use our product. There's nothing more gratifying than helping someone else turn a dream into a real business. And over time, we've found that our fulfillment comes as much from the process of trying to achieve our goals as it does from actually achieving them.

CHAPTER THREE

Plan Your Life, Then Plan Your Business

Stop Before You Go

ANTOINE—STARTUPNATION RADIO CALLER

We'll never forget a call we received on StartupNation Radio early in 2004. It was Antoine from Dallas. He was filled with vim and vigor and ready to work on his New Year's resolution to create a business that would allow him to achieve his primary objectives of spending more time with his kids and having more time to play golf. So we asked him if he had a specific business in mind that he believed would achieve his objectives. He replied by telling us he was thinking of a business to import specialty foods from various countries in Europe. Apparently he had an agent in Europe who would be his partner and take him around on buying trips to acquire unique food products that he could then, in turn, import to the United States to sell.

On the face of it, it sounded like a very interesting business. However, as we began to probe the details of what this business would require of him, Antoine disclosed that it would involve a great deal of time spent traveling overseas—the very time that he told us he wanted more of to spend with his kids and to play golf. We quickly surmised that if Antoine were to start that particular business, he would probably end up with even less time to lead the lifestyle he was seeking.

Antoine's story underscores the importance of knowing what kind of lifestyle you want to lead and then picking a business that facilitates your lifestyle objectives.

Right now, you might be working on the first prototype of your invention or you might be poring over the most recent draft of your business plan.

You're about to take the same step we took nearly two decades ago. You're about to turn your dream into a reality. We know this is an auspicious time, full of hope and planning, dreaming and doing.

For as long as we can remember, we wanted to do something with our lives that was truly done "our own way." Our grandfather, Sam, built his own scrap metal business when he landed on these shores in the 1930s as an immigrant who couldn't speak the language and had no more than a few dollars in his pocket. Our dad is a retired urologist and ran a practice on his own instead of joining in with physicians' groups. Our mom raised us to believe we didn't have to follow the traditional or conservative formula just because it was the way everyone else did it. She taught us to think big and to have confidence to do it our way. Add to this the experience of growing up in Flint. The city was wilting from General Motors' downsizing. Think Michael Moore's documentary *Roger and Me* set in Flint. For us, those were formative days. We just couldn't see ourselves "workin' for the man."

That's why we made a pact with each other that we'd do whatever it takes to lead a life rich with freedom, family, and fulfillment—ingredients that became integral to our Manifesto.

Can you relate? Perhaps a similar set of experiences has driven you to pick up this book—an intense family influence mixed with a desire to take control of your future and to answer only to yourself. No matter what's behind your interest in pursuing entrepreneurship, we know this moment—just before you really commit yourself to running your own business—is intense. If you're like most people, add generous amounts of fear and doubt to the mix. You're probably wondering about whether you're ready to take this big step. Will you really be able to make it on your own? Is being an entrepreneur in your blood? What will your family think? How will you finance the business without draining your personal savings? Will you be a success?

But before you travel any farther down the path to get your business started, put thoughts about "the business" on hold. There's something more important to think about first. We know a way to help you answer all those questions you're asking yourself and replace some of your doubt and uncertainty with confidence.

And it has nothing to do with business or your idea for that business or invention—yet. On the contrary, what we propose is something that's all too often overlooked by people thinking about starting up their own business. It's called *your life*. That's right. We want you to focus first on what you really want out of this new life you're about to create.

Why do we propose planning a life before planning a business?

We believe that you'll be most fulfilled by running your own show if you create a business that draws on what you really enjoy doing. You're going to spend a lot of time and energy to make a success of your new business. If you enjoy the work, you won't regret spending that time.

Using this approach, you'll find that the more you enjoy your work, the harder you're going to want to work. The harder you work, the closer you come to success.

This might seem like a radical notion: Plan your life before you've even researched your idea or written a business plan. At this point in most books, you'd start to dive into planning your business. We're going to get there too, but not before you know what you want. With a little bit of reflecting and envisioning, you can create a life that's totally fulfilling *and* create a business that serves that life. We think the founders of Great Harvest Bread Co., one of the most respected franchises in existence, said it perfectly in their biography, *Bread and Butter.* "Your business will always model your own physical and emotional health." We couldn't agree more.

Getting into the Mindset

First, know what you want. Too many people fall into a condition we call "drift," where, instead of taking life by the horns, they let life just kind of happen to them. It's easy to lull yourself into a state of drift, unaware of how wasteful it is to live this way. Make no mistake, drifting can delay—and even worse, prohibit—you from leading the life you want and deserve.

It might be helpful for you to look at life as a series of building blocks. The days are the blocks. Each layer of blocks depends on the layer below. And just like building blocks, tomorrow always depends on today and today upon yesterday, and so on and so on. Each day counts. When you drift, you're not building for tomorrow. The good news is that pulling yourself out of drift is actually simple. Your first step is to *create a Life Plan.*

Creating a Life Plan is a process we designed to help you understand who you are, what you *want* to do, what you *can* do, and how to get where you want to go. At this point, we recommend you grab a notebook and use it to record and organize your thoughts as we walk you through the steps. Ultimately, you'll be asked to organize your notes into a one- to two-page document titled "Life Plan." Once you have your Life Plan, you'll know how to spend each day moving toward your goal, and you'll know how different parts of your life serve your Life Plan, including your business.

First, what is a Life Plan?

A Life Plan is to your life what a business plan is to your business. It states where you want to go and what you have to do to get there. It lays out what you're trying to accomplish with your life, what rewards you'd like, and what the risks and costs will likely be. And it sets out a strategy for how to make it all happen. Your Life Plan is a guiding light that will keep you on course and free from "drift."

This Life Plan—revisited and rewritten at least annually—can help you make decisions about all aspects of your life. For example, you can use your Life Plan to figure out whether you should own a home or rent an apartment, whether you should have pets or not be tied down by that obligation, whether you should spend your money on material possessions now or set funds aside for retirement, or whether you should keep your corporate job or start up that dream business.

In the end, if you determine that your life would be best served by starting your own business, you'll use your Life Plan to help figure out the best type of business for you. Your Life Plan will literally drive your business plan, not vice versa.

When we look for shining examples of how people have created businesses in accordance with their Life Plans, all we have to do is look up and down our Main Street. Just down the way, Kate Richard, a 27-year-old successful entrepreneur, has mapped out a business that stirs her passion and affords her the privilege to do the kind of work she loves *every day*.

Kate always dreamed of owning a clothing store and living near her family. But like so many people, she feared that following those dreams seemed a little risky. So when she graduated from Miami University with a bachelor's degree in marketing, she headed first to Colorado and then San Francisco to work for big companies in their marketing departments. "I liked it well enough when I started, but I soon grew to despise it. I didn't have enough time to visit my family. I wasn't traveling like I wanted to," Kate says. Kate liked the work but wasn't happy with the life she was living.

So in December of 2002, she packed up her bags and headed home to Michigan. The plan was to spend a month with her family and then head back into the corporate world. "I thought I'd move to New York and land a marketing job there. At least I'd be in the same time zone with my family!"

But as she traveled in and out of New York during the interviewing process, Kate says she began to rethink her plans. "I wanted to be close to my family. I was really happy being near home. I knew I wanted more flexibility in my schedule and to have time to travel. I also knew I loved clothes and shopping. All I needed was a way to make a living."

What Kate did was to make her lifestyle the top priority, then figure out a way to mold a business that would fit her lifestyle. She put her Life Plan before her business plan.

As Kate looked around town, filled with curiosity and interest in the businesses she saw, she began to realize that the possibilities for a career were broader than simply heading back into the corporate world. What if she opened her own store selling clothes? It occurred to her that not only would she be dealing with fashion, but she'd have perfect justification to travel—frequenting fashion shows and the great cities of the world to find the best merchandise. The solution was staring her in the face, and it was not a "job" at all: She could open her own clothing store in downtown Birmingham.

"After that thought hit me, I quickly abandoned the idea of going off to New York and hunting for a job in the fashion industry. Once I started thinking of doing my own thing, I couldn't shake the idea. I wanted to create a space—*my space*—where it would be fun to shop for clothes."

Thus the store Miss Kate was born. When you step inside, it's obvious that she's created a business that melds her dream life with her skills. On one wall is a big plasma television screen playing chick flicks. The clothes are organized by colors instead of by designers, since "it's easier to shop that way." Along the back wall is a fireplace with couches and chairs facing it to create a warm, comfortable living space. While she's still working 14-hour days, with the manager she has on board, she's able to take off days to spend with her family. And it's not uncommon for her sister and parents to drop by the shop, just minutes from their homes. She often travels to places like London and New York to meet with vendors, find the best lines, and cut deals.

The melding of her Life Plan with her business plan is paying off. She's expanded with a bridesmaid's salon at the back of Miss Kate and also opened a new store, Shoe La La, across the street. Next move? "I'd love to have a few more stores like Miss Kate around the country."

A Life Plan of Your Own

To get you started on your own Life Plan, first understand there's no one "right" way to do it. Second, be aware that your plan will not stay the same forever. It'll morph and change numerous times just as our plans have over the years. Life has a way of doing that. Your task is to think through the issues we highlight *before* you become consumed with the details of the business you're going to start. The important thing is to be thoughtful and honest with yourself, and to be open to the unexpected. The work you do in this section of *StartupNation* might save you from heading down the wrong path or from heading down the right one but running out of steam just months after starting up.

You'll need to be both a dreamer and a realist throughout this process. Once you've worked your way through it, you should finally be equipped to distill all of your thoughts and notes into a "Life Plan" that you can literally live by. It'll be invaluable in helping you become not only a successful entrepreneur but a more fulfilled person.

Here's what you'll address in our six-step life-planning process:

1. Your Current Status
2. Your Ideal Life
3. Your Skills: What You Do Well
4. Your Ideal Work Style
5. Your Manifesto
6. Your Key Moves

One or two pages is about the right length. You can find a sample of a Life Plan near the end of this section.

For an online form you can use to create and maintain your own Life Plan, go to www.startupnation.com/lifeplan.

Step 1—Establish Your Current Status

Rate Your Quality of Life

The first thing to do when creating your Life Plan is to take stock of your current situation. Granted, it's impossible for you to be completely objective, but try to be as candid as possible. To improve anything in your life, you have to know where you stand today. Start by simply rating your quality of life on a scale from 1 to 100, with 100 being the best possible life you can imagine. Ask yourself some simple questions:

Is life good? Where do you stand relative to your ideal? How close? How far? Are you excited to wake up and start the day? Are your relationships in good standing? Do you have enough time to yourself? Do you smile and laugh a lot? Do you feel happy? Successful? Fulfilled? Think about life in its most basic components—work, play, relationships, finances. Give each a rating. You may score very high in some areas and low in others. While it's crucial to think about everything you want to do with your life in the future, it's just as important to know what it is about your life *right now* that makes you happy or unhappy.

Analyze Your Reality

Is your overall score a wake-up call that you're squandering your precious time? Has drift gotten the best of you? If you gave your quality of life a low rating, don't let it become a self-fulfilling prophecy that influences how you rate it in the future. Whatever you do, remember that this rating is only a snapshot in time, and it should only improve with each day going forward. You have the power to change it, and with careful planning and commitment, you'll get there.

Note: We're not suggesting that you should change anything about your life. You may be right where you want to be, and that's perfectly fine. The objective is simply to examine your current standing and evaluate whether or not it's working for you.

Every time we rate the quality of our lives, we start by harkening back to an old Chinese story that you might find helpful, too.

THE STONECUTTER

There was once a stonecutter, who was dissatisfied with himself and with his position in life.

One day, he passed a wealthy merchant's house, and through the open gateway, saw many fine possessions and important visitors. "How powerful that merchant must be!" thought the stonecutter. He became very envious, and wished that he could be like the merchant. Then he would no longer have to live the life of a mere stonecutter.

(continued on next page)

To his great surprise, he suddenly became the merchant, enjoying more luxuries and power than he had ever dreamed of, envied and detested by those less wealthy than himself. But soon a high official passed by, carried in a sedan chair, accompanied by attendants, and escorted by soldiers beating gongs. Everyone, no matter how wealthy, had to bow low before the procession. "How powerful that official is!" he thought. "I wish that I could be a high official!"

Then he became the high official, carried everywhere in his embroidered sedan chair, feared and hated by the people all around, who had to bow down before him as he passed. It was a hot summer day, and the official felt very uncomfortable in the sticky sedan chair. He looked up at the sun. It shone proudly in the sky, unaffected by his presence. "How powerful the sun is!" he thought. "I wish that I could be the sun!"

Then he became the sun, shining fiercely down on everyone, scorching the fields, cursed by the farmers and laborers. But a huge black cloud moved between him and the earth, so that his light could no longer shine on everything below. "How powerful that storm cloud is!" he thought. "I wish that I could be a cloud!"

Then he became the cloud, flooding the fields and villages, shouted at by everyone. But soon he found that he was being pushed away by some great force, and realized that it was the wind. "How powerful it is!" he thought. "I wish that I could be the wind!"

Then he became the wind, blowing tiles off the roofs of houses, uprooting trees, hated and feared by all below him. But after a while, he ran up against something that would not move, no matter how forcefully he blew against it—a huge towering stone. "How powerful that stone is!" he thought. "I wish that I could be a stone!"

Then he became the stone, more powerful than anything else on earth. But as he stood there, he heard the sound of a hammer pounding a chisel into the solid rock, and felt himself being changed. "What could be more powerful than I, the stone?" he thought. He looked down and saw far below him the figure of a stonecutter.

—*The Tao of Pooh*, by Benjamin Hoff

This tale of self-awareness speaks volumes about the need to reflect on the life you're already living before you begin to create a new one for yourself as an entrepreneur.

Consider the Impact on Your Relationships. How important are your family and friends? Do they come first? Your relationships with others will no doubt be affected if you become an entrepreneur. And you won't find true happiness unless you account for them as you begin to formulate your plans. We've heard many times the story of the entrepreneur who weathers all the entrepreneurial storms and builds a successful business but loses a marriage or key friendships, or time that could have been spent with children.

This doesn't have to happen.

To make sure you protect this most important part of your life, start by considering the responsibilities you have to other people in your life—to your spouse, your friends, your children. Carve out time for them. Make it a priority if it's important to you.

One entrepreneur who carefully considered her family responsibilities before designing her ideal business is solo entrepreneur Joan Isabella.

THE STORY OF YO! RADIO, INC.

We met Joan Isabella in 2003 when we were looking for someone to help us with our live StartupNation radio show. Joan and her radio consulting firm Yo! Radio were well known in Detroit. At one point, she was the executive producer of the nationally syndicated radio show for Mitch Albom, author of the best-selling *Tuesdays with Morrie* and *The Five People You Meet in Heaven* and a sports columnist for the *Detroit Free Press*.

Recognizing that her family life was central to her Life Plan, she'd created her dream business (Yo! Radio) in a setup that worked perfectly for her. She not only was working in her favorite medium, with one of

(continued on next page)

the best-known authors and journalists in America, but she could manage her own schedule. How? With Yo! Radio, she works as an independent contractor. In this way, she can work full-time on one account, as she did for a while with Mitch Albom, or she can work on several accounts, as she does today. StartupNation is one of her clients. She has the flexibility to regulate how much she works at any one time by regulating how many clients she consults with.

Following the birth of her son, Daniel, Joan was able to work from home so that she could raise her son while doing her work. Joan lives this dream life today because she knew what she wanted out of life, what her priorities were, and she had a plan for how to make it all work.

Joan's story really reinforces the value of life planning. By making the decision that raising Daniel would be her priority, she set up a framework for what kind of business she could entertain. She took out all the travel, and took on only those customers who could respect her limited availability.

Instead of consulting for 40 hours a week, she limited her workload to 10 hours a week, all from home. Unlike women who have built careers inside corporations, Joan didn't have to decide between her work and her child. Instead, she let family be a huge part of her business decisions.

Just like Joan, one out of 11 women in America have designed their own dream businesses, often balancing family responsibilities with entrepreneurial ambitions, and the number grows every year.

Get Frank About Your Financials. To gain peace of mind when dealing with the financial realities that come with starting a business, you have to be honest with yourself about your current finances and future needs. This is a vital part of the self-portrait you're painting.

First, develop a list of fixed personal expenses. Include everything that's important, and we mean everything. Tackle the big monthly payments first. Mortgage or rent, health insurance, food and clothing, car payments, car insurance, monthly retirement allocations, taxes. You get the idea. Remember your responsibilities: If you've got a parent, a spouse, and children counting on you, factor their needs into this category. Total these items. The number you'll end up with is your baseline. It's what you *have to* earn to meet your obligations.

Now consider your variable expenses—things you choose to pay for versus things you have to pay for. Things like entertainment, recreation, travel, hobbies, and interests. Remember, these expenses can be managed. You can rein in this spending when necessary and start spending again when you're confident you can cover the costs. Combine variable expenses with the fixed expenses and add a little extra as a rainy-day fund for contingencies or emergencies. Now you know how much money you'll need on the personal side while you're starting and growing your business. Being clear on this will help you enjoy the journey instead of stressing out.

Once you've got a handle on your financial needs, analyze what your sources of money are. First, do a rundown of all your current sources of cash. Maybe you've tucked away a nice savings account that you're willing to use for a business. Or maybe you're bullish on using your credit cards or a home-equity line. If so, put a number on the amount you'd be able to tap. Then list income from investments and any part-time or full-time salary that you or your spouse will be earning from other work during the startup phase of your business.

Next, figure out what assets you have that can be converted to cash, including investments, personal goods, and so on. You may be forced to consider this option before you get started in order to cover your needs. In assembling this list, rank the assets in order of how liquid they are and what their corresponding cash value will likely be upon liquidation. Lastly, consider outside sources of capital if they'll be needed. These sources include friends and family, and angel investors, covered in Chapter Six.

Now you've quantified and qualified what money is *really*

FAST FACT: ENTREPRENEURIAL INCOME

The average business owner makes an estimated $112,800 a year. That's more than twice as much as the annual salary of non-executive employees and far above the median household income in the United States. If you're anywhere near "average" as an entrepreneur, then most likely you'll be able to pay those monthly bills and a whole lot more.

Source: *Inc.* magazine, December 2003

---

available to you currently and in the year ahead. When we begin the business planning in Chapter Five, these figures will allow you to design a business that takes into account your personal needs.

At the conclusion of this stage of life planning, you should have your arms around where you are in life. You should have some insight about what makes you happy and what gets you down, about what's working in your life and what's not. You'll be more attuned to your relationships with others and more clearheaded about your financial situation. Now that you have some important fundamentals accounted for, you can free yourself to think about the future. You can think about *you*.

You're in a place to consider the possibilities that exist beyond your current reality. And that starts with a good dose of daydreaming.

Step 2—Create Your Ideal Life

Do Some Blue-Sky Thinking. Look forward. What do you see?

Do you see yourself running a flower shop on the corner? Do you see yourself traveling in South America, working with indigenous people? Working as a fashion designer in Manhattan? A farmer selling exotic chili peppers through your online store?

Think about your vision. Picture yourself in old age and work your way back. Perhaps you retired early to play golf or to see faraway countries. Maybe you moved to the town where your grandchildren live so you could spend time with them each week.

It could be that you left an extraordinary legacy in your community, creating jobs and sponsoring Little League teams. Or your legacy could be even more grandiose—you changed the lives of thousands of people for the better with your innovation in personal safety. Maybe your ideal life resulted in your making a mint, with a penthouse apartment in the city and you playing the role of Daddy Warbucks.

The sky's the limit. That's why we're asking you to do "blue-sky thinking," no matter how overcast your current reality may be. Whatever you do, don't be shy or timid—*it's your future!* So be true to what you want for yourself.

Looking backward from old age, imagine how you'd live today if life were ideal. How much of every day would you spend at work versus with family and friends? If material possessions are important, decide which ones would bring you closer to your dream life and what you have to do to get them. As part of this, consider the type of work that you'd love to throw yourself at— the kind that invigorates you rather than wears you out.

You Gotta Love It. We often have the privilege of speaking at universities on the subject of entrepreneurship and innovation. Our talks with the undergrads are particularly thrilling for us. There's something really exciting about catching young people when they're still wide-eyed. They're not burdened with grad-school student loans, nor have they been boxed into a specific career path. They're still free to imagine and explore the possibilities ahead of them. Over the years, we've noticed an odd phenomenon: At the end of many of these speeches, one of the more outgoing under-grads will often approach us and say, "I want your life."

And while of course this is a stunning thing to hear, we understand what they *really* mean. They want a life lived *their* way, just as we live ours our way. They want a life led according to their own vision. They want a life filled with achievement and pride. We understand that none of this is easy, and it's not for everyone. We're on airplanes a lot, sometimes with stops in three cities a week. We put in exceedingly long hours. We deal with the daily pressure of knowing a decision we make today or an action we take tomorrow may be the difference between making it big and sheer doom. We relish spending some weekends in the office instead of being on the golf course. This extra time in the office is time for us to write articles, prep for our radio show, think about our business without being interrupted by phone calls, and work on crafting business plans and strategies for new startups at Sloan Ventures. We even schedule meetings in the evenings and on weekends with our staff and with the entrepreneurs we work with to build our companies. The bottom line is that we're doing what we love. We thrive on this excitement. It's the lifestyle we want to live. We find it exciting, whereas no doubt others would see it as overwhelming.

We determined a long time ago that we love the buzz and the excitement of the beginning stages of running a business, those first heady months of entrepreneurship. People respond passionately to the idea that we can consciously choose a path that fits our dreams, stick to that path, and, no matter what challenges come up, make our work serve our ideal life. One of our close advisors once told us that "if you love your work, you'll never work a day in your life." We've lived this way for years, and it has made our ideal life *work*.

We both have personal dreams and interests we pursue every day that have nothing to do with "the business." For Jeff that means playing classical guitar or riding his horse. For Rich it's sculpting steel and teaching yoga classes. We both love our golden retrievers and the pure joy of hanging out with them.

Our relationships with our parents and our sister's family are also important to us. Our parents often fly in from Phoenix, armed with pertinent business-oriented newspaper clips they've collected. When we're near Phoenix, and by that we mean any time we're west of the Mississippi River, we often book a connecting flight through there just to spend time with them. And, if we're lucky, we even throw in a stop in Chicago to spend time with our niece and nephew. We hope to have families of our own one day and dedicate our focus to them. But for the time being we've designed our individual life plans to focus on building our business first.

Knowing and honoring the things that are important to us have been instrumental in fashioning the gratifying life we lead. To help you enjoy this same degree of contentment—filling your life with the elements you love—consider questions like the following: If you had an afternoon off, how would you spend it? When do you feel most alive? What courses did you particularly enjoy in school? What activities do you lose yourself in? What gives you a sense of accomplishment?

Choosing to be an entrepreneur is more of a life decision than a business decision. So when it's time to start designing your business, make sure you take your answers to these questions into account. Make sure you stay true to who you are and what's important to you. This concept began to take root in us when we were growing up. We read Richard Bach's book *Jonathan Livingston Seagull*, a classic fable about finding your passions and your true self. In the story, Jonathan doesn't see himself just as another bird. Nor does he view flying as some humdrum, practical activity he does every day simply to find food. Instead, he sees it as an *art form*—one worthy of perfecting. Jonathan loved to fly! And so, staying true to what he loved, Jonathan did it his way. Yes—he had to endure ridicule from the rest of the flock. But in the end he transformed their ridicule into respect. Most important, he transformed what would have been an average, unimaginative life into one of real contentment. Like Jonathan, we're certainly doing things our own way. We're inspired to question what we're doing with our daily lives, in our work and beyond. We challenge ourselves to be conscious and artful. And you should, too.

What will your art form be? If you think it might be living your days as an entrepreneur, make sure your reasons are substantial and sound. You should understand that, by becoming an entrepreneur, you will not become someone else, but more *yourself*. Be clear on where you want to go. You'll have to make sacrifices; make sure in the end that these sacrifices don't cost you your happiness.

Be True to Yourself

Jeff: Neither of us has ever held a day job in the traditional sense. I've never received a salary from any source that I didn't create myself. I didn't even make it through the first day of law school. I'd given out the school's number to the attorney who was working on securing our license agreement for our invention, the Battery Buddy. We were very close to closing the deal, and the reality is that I never really wanted to be a lawyer in the first place. I had enrolled only as a fallback to my real dream of being an entrepreneur. In my second class of the first day, a school secretary came by the classroom and announced that I had received an important phone call. It was my lawyer. I excused myself from class and took the call. He informed me that our terms were accepted and that the deal would close. Immediately following the call, I returned to class, picked up my books, returned to the registrar's office where I had just a few hours earlier officially enrolled, and announced that I would be leaving law school. I was granted the distinction of "the fastest ever to withdraw."

Now, truth be told, though I made this move with great bravado, looking back on it I can confess I was full of fear. But most important, I was excited. I was pursuing life as an entrepreneur, doing it my way! Certainly I respect those who are lawyers and those who are employed by others. The point, however, is that you should do what works for you.

Do You Have What It Takes?

In our experience, if you're even considering starting up a business, you've probably got the entrepreneurial spirit running through your veins. The fact is, you'll never really know until you *put yourself to the test.* If you have passion for your idea—the kind of passion that wakes you up in the middle of the night with strategies to market your product or land a new client—it's a sure sign that you're an entrepreneur.

If you're dealing with the fear of failure, don't let that deter you. Get comfortable with the idea that as a business owner, you're going to fail sometimes—that's a given. Failure's not all bad as long as you can learn from it. Remember the old adage: Nothing ventured, nothing gained. Being able to fail, recover, and keep right on going is a valuable trait for any entrepreneur to have.

We failed the first time we applied for a patent for the Battery Buddy, and we've failed in plenty of other ways, as well. But those failures drove us to get smarter, to work harder, and then drove us to new heights in our business careers.

Our good friend Tom Crum knows the silver lining of failure. Tom consults with major corporations on stress management, conflict resolution, and team building through his organization Aiki Works in Aspen, Colorado, and has written a book called *The Magic of Conflict.* Tom suggests that conflict and failure are not only inevitable but actually something that should be embraced. It's during times of conflict that we learn and grow the most. Tom writes:

Since so often what we observe in crisis is people in struggle, pain, and fear, is it any wonder that our ordinary reaction becomes a confused combination of those elements? There is an alternative—a way of responding to crisis that is extraordinary. Integrating this approach will enable you to bring forth a life of power, freedom, and joy. Using pressure, change, and the unknown, an artist can sculpt a masterpiece. Seeing conflict as an opportunity to create art from our very being is a challenge for the artist in all of us. Our lives are not dependent on whether or not we will have conflict. It is what we do with conflict that makes the difference.

Dealing with failure is one thing. Natural entrepreneurial ability is quite another. You may be thinking—and rightly so—that some people just seem to be born with more natural entrepreneurial ability than others. To figure out whether or not you have this natural edge, ask yourself the following questions:

Did you grow up among entrepreneurial family members? Many of the entrepreneurs we've met have entrepreneurial parents. That's not surprising. Studies show that more than 60 percent of successful entrepreneurs have at least one parent who is or was self-employed.

It certainly was the case for us.

Our dad worked to pay his own way through college and medical school. But he chose not to go the safe "strength in numbers" way when he started practicing medicine. Instead of joining a physicians' group, he stayed independent, running his own very successful practice. Working closely with our mom, he did his own marketing, ran his own staff, established his own customer service philosophy, and, like a true entrepreneur, adopted innovative new technologies that enhanced patient care. No one worked harder—we never saw him miss a day of work. Most of the time, he was up and out of the house before we woke up to go to school. Our dad went on to become a recognized pioneer of new techniques, and while he threw more hours at his work than anyone else we knew, there was no end to the passion he had for what he was doing. By watching and listening to our dad, we learned it was possible to take risks and succeed in a big way.

Our mom taught us to be aware and to be sensitive to what was working and what was not working in the consumer world. She often commented on a television commercial she felt was effective or a new product she believed would sell well or even what movies, celebrities, or songs she thought would make it in the current pop-culture environment. She talked about the great thinkers and significant inventions. She maintained a constant sense of awareness and was always analyzing things. And she was always encouraging us to do the same.

Our father's pioneering ways and work ethic combined with our mother's sensitivity and awareness to the world around us were a powerful influence for us as budding entrepreneurs. We were taught to be open to possibilities, to think in creative and individual ways, and to work harder than anybody else.

Were you the eldest? Studies from both Harvard and Columbia Universities reveal that 70 percent of entrepreneurs are firstborn children. If you're a second or third child with six years separating you from your oldest sibling, you're also more likely to be entrepreneurial. (Yes, we fit that bill—seven years separate us.)

Were you entrepreneurial as a child? Did you have a lemonade stand? Were you always thinking of ways to make a little extra spending money? Did you dream up businesses that you could run with your siblings or friends? Those early endeavors, probably long forgotten, are telltale signs that somewhere inside you is an entrepreneur-in-waiting.

How do you cope when you're challenged? Extreme challenges are a reality in life. They're certainly also a reality when running your own business. As an entrepreneur, you'll be put to the test like never before. And many times, there'll be no obvious way to prevail. You'll have to be determined and resourceful. You'll have to be a creative problem solver. And you'll have to accept the fact that you won't always succeed. As Tom Crum would say, you'll have to find the magic in the negatives and use them to move you forward. With that spirit guiding you, you'll be thinking like the most successful of entrepreneurs.

Do you have a burning passion? While it's great to be born with natural ability, to be the oldest child, to have entrepreneurial parents, or to be blessed with whatever other qualities may lead to being a successful entrepreneur, we know that having a burning passion supersedes all else. Having a fire in your belly may be the single most important determining factor as to whether or not you have what it takes to start and grow a successful business. There's no such thing as "entitlement" in the world of entrepreneurship. Regardless of natural ability, we believe that anyone can be an entrepreneur as long as they have a burning passion, the right knowledge, and a desire to put what they've learned into action.

Step 3—Compare Your Skills to Your Passions

Play to Your Strength. Building a business requires a wide range of skills and talents, and few of us are good at all of them. The key is to know your strengths, play to them, and round out your team with those who can fill critical roles better than you can. When we set out to build a new business, we do it knowing that we each have distinct talents. To explain these strengths in business, we often tell the story of how the two of us would build a road through a jungle. It goes something like this.

Jeff

I, Jeff, armed with a giant machete, would size up the forest ahead and be able to see the way through it to the other side. Driven by my vision, I'd begin by hacking my way into the dense green foliage to create a clearing for a road through the jungle. I have only one thought in mind: How do I get to the other side? I see the end, not necessarily all the steps along the way. I knock down the biggest trees and enough of the underbrush to leave a rugged path for others to follow. When I'm done, you can see through the jungle, which, until I came along, was a dense thicket of unexplored territory. But, I'd admit, with all the snaking vines and big logs in the way, it's still not yet a road.

Rich

That's where I, Rich, come in. I'm the "road builder." I like to pull out the stumps, smooth the hills, excavate the drainage ditches, lay down a nice, thick coat of asphalt, and then paint a dashed white line down the middle of the road to make it easy to navigate. Then I'd probably end up proposing that we locate a tollbooth at the beginning and end of the road, to make it a profitable venture!

So now you get a sense of how we'd break down our roles—the difference in how we each apply our passion and our skills. That's not to say that we couldn't do each other's jobs. But we have our true strengths, and we're at our best when we play to them. Neither one of us could've built a road without the other. While the big vision is what's particularly interesting to Jeff, making it happen is what Rich enjoys. Our partnership is what makes us successful.

Figuring out what your strengths are (and your weaknesses) can be a very revealing exercise. If you ultimately decide to launch your own business, you'll have the opportunity to do everything inside your company, from strategizing about how to land the next big customer to changing the lightbulbs. Knowing your skills will help you better craft—and probably narrow—the role you'll take in your business. By understanding what your weaknesses are—what makes you cringe with reluctance or fear—you'll keep yourself from taking on those tasks and, instead, have others who are more qualified handle them. If you don't, you'll likely end up with mediocre performance and a business that's in jeopardy.

To help us pull this concept together, we enlisted our ever-helpful chief community officer at StartupNation, Joel Welsh. Prior to this role, Joel was a headhunter and a recruiter for almost 20 years. He's helped thousands of people, especially those within the corporate ranks, identify their strengths.

It might seem easy to just list what you know how to do. Perhaps you write computer code, for example, or you like selling things. Joel recommends that you write out a list of your greatest accomplishments. Accomplishments, for this purpose, are any career-related activities that have given you a sense of satisfaction. They may be big or small. They can range from award-winning efforts to everyday tasks you consistently did well over time. They may be things that you did alone or as a member of a team.

Try to come up with at least five, but it can certainly be more than that. Think about the accomplishments. What did it take to actually achieve them? What skills did you draw upon to achieve recognition or to get the job done well?

The purpose of the exercise is to translate the strengths and skills you use when you've been at your best into strengths and skills that you should apply if you decide to build a new business. Joel's keys to writing an accomplishment statement:

- Always start with—or at least include—an action verb.
- Include enough important details to make it interesting, including quantitative data (numbers, amounts, and percentages).
- Do one of the following: (1) Start with actions you took followed by results you achieved, (2) start with results achieved followed by actions taken, or (3) simply describe in some detail significant job functions you performed.

To show how this exercise works, we asked Joel to provide his own accomplishment statement. After reading it, you'll have a great picture of his skills *and* you'll see why we love having Joel on our team.

My Accomplishments and the Skills It Took to Achieve Them

1. Built personalized database of 14,000 business professionals throughout the United States one person at a time. This database provided a community of new business prospects and candidates for the successful completion of recruiting projects, allowing for the growth and sustaining of my own recruiting practice for 19 years. Skills: Initiative, imagination, innovation, leadership.

2. Established business relationships with 5,000 eNewsletter recipients through the creation of a content-rich website of career-counseling and job-search assistance. Maintained over a 98 percent retention rate of eNewsletter recipients even though this was an opt-out subscriber base. Skills: Innovation, imagination.

3. Developed and ran a basketball outreach ministry at my local church, which included over 200 young men during a ten-year

period, reaching across racial and traditional socio-economic barriers. Skills: Leadership, vision, initiative, listening.

4. Provided family leadership during my mom's four-year battle with cancer and dad's life-threatening hepatitis C and brain surgery, while living 500 miles from the rest of the family. Took the lead on directing both to nationally recognized top-tier hospitals for care that were out-of-state (Johns Hopkins and University of Pittsburgh Medical Center). Skills: Problem solving, leadership, initiative, listening, persuasion, interpretation.

5. Took up playing baseball (men's hardball) at age 39 after a 24-year layoff. Hit for a .400 average in my second season. Was third baseman on team that won men's national championship in the 28-year-old division in my third season and was asked to manage the team the following season. Skills: Initiative, imagination, problem solving.

It Takes Skill. Now let's look at four major skills and what types of businesses work well with each.

Great selling skills: If this defines you, you probably like people, interacting with them, and maintaining relationships with them. You also don't mind rejection, seeing it simply as part of the process of selling. You have a willingness to overcome the "No"s that come your way. You're able to think on your feet and present yourself well in public. You like the short-term rush of landing the deal. Sales reps, real estate agents, insurance agents—all entrepreneurs in their own rights—are experts in sales.

Marketing skills: You know how to appeal to people's needs and wants. You're intuitive and able to hit the hot buttons with people. You're strategic and like seeing your ideas make it to the market, even if it takes a long time. You know how to get to the heart of the customer. Creating a new brand, opening up a retail store, or consulting in marketing and public relations would be good routes for someone with these skills.

Creative skills: You thrive on creativity. You like solving problems and are constantly coming up with ideas. These ideas could fall in the scientific or artistic realms. But trying to sell the products you think up or marketing them doesn't necessarily drive you. You like the process of invention. Ad agencies are built around this kind of skill, as are web development and graphic design firms.

Analytical skills: You enjoy thinking through existing systems and processes and making them work better. Businesses that involve real estate management and development, manufacturing, financial advice, or consulting to larger enterprises all draw heavily on analytical skills, as do professions like law and accounting.

When you think deeply about this, you'll discover where you're strong—and if you're honest about it, you'll also carve out some areas where you're clearly weak and unskilled. Remember, don't try to be Superman here! This is about being true to yourself, dealing with who you are and who you aren't. Always play to your strength.

Are You Experienced? On that note, be sure to take into account areas where you have experience. If you've managed a big team within a corporation, this is very meaningful. You may take it for granted because it's old hat to you, but the fact is, there are lots of nuances and tons of tricks of the trade that you pick up *just by doing.* Maybe you've spent a few years selling at retail— perhaps selling shoes, as our dad did as a teenager at Macy's—or as a waitress in the hospitality industry. Include any area where you've accumulated a valuable track record. It could even be at a charitable level as a leader in a community-service organization like the Rotary Club.

As you record what your base of experience is, it might feel like you're writing a résumé. And we know that while you might have experience doing certain things, it's those very things you might also be tired of and want to avoid doing in the future. So if your reflex is to kick and scream as you're forced through this process, that's totally understandable. Stay tuned in to that sentiment if you feel it. And don't worry. We're going to make sure you don't fall back into leading a life that's anything but *exactly what you want*.

Step 4—Your Ideal Work Style

We're well into the life-planning process of gathering the info you'll use to determine *when* and *how* you'll pursue the life of an entrepreneur. If you can resist just a little longer, try to keep your specific business idea on the back burner. Taking into account your current reality, your vision of an ideal life, and your passions, strengths, skills, and experience, now's the time to figure out your work style—how much risk you are willing to take and how many hours you're willing to put in.

It's About Time. How many hours each week are you really willing to spend working? Think about this relative to other priorities you've already considered as part of the life-planning process, such as family, friends, and perhaps leisure travel. It's important to be disciplined and reality-based. Come up with a range—whether it's five or 50 hours a week, just pick the number of hours you think you could stick to. It might help to start by answering the following questions:

YOUR WORK LIFE

1. What are the priorities in your life that rank higher than work? How does that affect the time you can spend running a business?
2. How would you spend the day working if you could plan your own work hours?

3. Would you work in a traditional office or work at home?

4. How many days would you have off each year?

Given the statistics about small-business owners working more than 50 hours a week on average, answering these questions might seem pointless. But look closer and you'll find that, unlike people on the corporate path, business owners choose *which* 50 hours they want to work. Or, in the case of the part-time entrepreneur, which five hours they want to work. Also, many of them are doing exactly what they want to be doing, so while there's certainly stress to deal with, as a business owner you can end the day more energized than when you started. We hear from many entrepreneurs who've left the corporate world that they'd take the stress of running their own business any day over the stress of working within a big corporation on things they're not passionate about and having to report to a boss who treats them like a number.

Establish Your Risk Profile. Now decide how much you're willing to risk and how much you *can* risk in starting a business.

The world seems to revere people who put it on the line. We certainly do—but only when the risks are taken in a calculated way. One of our favorite real-life risk-takers is Cyrus Field, featured in the book *A Thread Across the Ocean*. Field conceived and then funded the laying of the world's first telegraph cable under the Atlantic Ocean in the mid-1800s. Despite experimental technology, numerous failed attempts, and personal and financial disasters, Field persevered and tied two continents together. He connected the old and new worlds so that news could travel instantaneously between the continents instead of requiring weeks of shipborne delivery. For his century, it was the technological equivalent of landing a man on the moon. The mountain of risk he overcame was dwarfed only by his planning and courage.

There are, of course, many more examples of risk-takers. Michael Dell and Bill Gates took the risk of dropping out of school and going for broke. Other entrepreneurs seem to jump feet-first into the most outlandish and unexpected ventures, like Virgin Group's Richard Branson, who's gone from running Virgin Records to Virgin Airlines to selling Virgin soda and cell phones.

Though on the surface it may seem otherwise, in fact, most successful entrepreneurs are calculated risk-takers; rather than being wildly impulsive, they build a rationale for taking the risk. Michael Dell started selling his computers when he was a freshman at the University of Texas in Austin. He stopped going to classes his sophomore year—once he had momentum in his budding business, not before. Richard Branson has been even more calculating. He didn't expand his Virgin brand to other business niches until Virgin Airlines had brand recognition among millions of consumers around the globe.

Do you find your mind racing as you read about these bold entrepreneurs? Are you asking yourself if *you* have what it takes? If you're willing to *risk it all*? For us, taking on bold, risky initiatives is just part of the way we live.

A perfect example is what we did with Clarity Technologies, a company we developed at Sloan Ventures back in 1997 in partnership with an extraordinary scientist/entrepreneur, Gail Erten, PhD. The idea behind Clarity was to commercialize innovative software technology that, among other things, would eliminate background noise during cell phone conversations. Today, Clarity has customers ranging from IBM and Motorola to Daimler-Chrysler and is truly a success story.

When we look back on the early days of launching the company, we often think about the put-everything-on-the-line moves we had to make to ensure that Clarity would survive its childhood. There were many times when the company, as a pioneer in a market that was still in its formative stages, came close to vaporizing. One of those moments stands out above others as an example of how taking bold, yet calculated, risks can be the difference between success and failure. We were confronted with a do-or-die decision—the company was within days of running out of cash. We could either let the company run out of money and implode, or step into the role of financiers to rescue the company— something, frankly, we weren't financially equipped to do at the time. It would require us to drain our personal savings.

Prior to this crisis, we had created a strategy that would provide the company with capital invested by a very smart and financially capable angel investor whom we'll call L.P. At the time, L.P. agreed to provide early "matching funding," which was critical in order to secure SBIR funding from the government.

FAST FACT: FEDERAL FUNDING

Small Business Innovative Research (SBIR) funding is provided to private companies by government agencies such as the Department of Defense and the National Science Foundation. The money is used for research that has potential utility for the sponsoring agency, and at the same time it allows the recipient companies to develop the research for their own commercial applications. Visit www.sba.gov/sbir to find out about SBIR funding.

As part of the SBIR funding Clarity was seeking, there was a time-sensitive opportunity to establish "fast-track" funding that would provide four government dollars for every one dollar provided by a private investor—in this case, L.P. We wanted to use this fast-track opportunity as a way to mitigate L.P.'s investment risk as much as possible but still get Clarity the money it needed.

The deal we made with L.P. was for him to invest an additional, prearranged amount of money each time the company achieved another performance milestone. It was a way to mitigate risk for L.P. and served as an added incentive for Clarity to perform. The SBIR fast-track funding was dependent in part on getting L.P.'s matching investment at each of these milestones. So the idea was to have Gail Erten, the founder, achieve five key milestones, each of which would trigger the obligation of L.P. to invest the next round, which in turn would trigger the availability of the grant money. The plan was perfect. Or so we thought.

Gail breezed through the first couple of milestones, and everything worked exactly according to plan. However, on the third milestone, there was, let's say, some "gray area" about whether or not the milestone had been achieved. And L.P., justifiably, questioned whether or not it had been achieved. With the deadline just a few days away, L.P. flew in on his private jet to have a sit-down meeting. We pored over Gail's data. Still a gray area. We had experts evaluate the data. Still a gray area. And the deadline to provide the government with proof that we'd secured the next round of matching funds was fast approaching.

On the last day before the deadline, we were in Atlanta meeting with another investor we were trying to enlist in case L.P. didn't make the critical payment. While this investor expressed interest, he claimed he would need weeks to make his decision. That clearly wasn't going to work.

We were in a tough spot.

We headed for the airport to catch a flight back to Detroit. As we heard the gate attendant make the last call for passengers to board the plane, we were still frantically working the pay phones.

"Gail, can you come up with any more specific data?"

"L.P. . . . are you sure you can't feel comfortable going ahead based on the data we have?"

Both answered, "No." And in that moment, Clarity's fate hung in the balance. As we reluctantly boarded the plane, we discovered we were assigned seats on different sides of the plane. We glanced at each other from across the aisle knowing what we had to do. As the flight attendant made the preflight announcement, we made two last calls from the airplane back-of-seat phone. The first was to our banker. We instructed her to wire our hard-earned personal savings directly to Clarity in order to secure the SBIR funding. The second call was to Gail, whom we advised to get verification of the wire transfer from our banker and then immediately inform the government that the required investment had been made prior to the deadline. With the phones finally turned off, we acknowledged each other over the heads of our fellow passengers and sank back into our seats exhilarated.

The end result: Clarity received the fast-track SBIR funding. Months later, once the data clearly indicated the performance milestone had indeed been achieved, L.P. ended up reimbursing us for our investment. Everyone was happy, and Clarity was on its way. Once again, a calculated risk had paid off. To this day, Clarity Technologies remains one of our best-performing companies, one that wouldn't exist had it not been for true entrepreneurial risk-taking.

Step 5—Making Your Own Manifesto

A manifesto is a declaration of intentions or principles. If you're an entrepreneur, it's what guides you in business. Since life planning is designed to help you understand the type of life that'll bring you happiness and fulfillment, establishing your own manifesto is instrumental. It'll provide context to what you do. It'll act as a reminder of why you're taking risks and working so hard. It'll help you keep perspective during times of challenge and opportunity. It'll make you focus on what's meaningful.

To create a personal manifesto, start by probing your most fundamental intentions and principles. What you find may or may not be the stereotypical "I'm in it for the money." If you're anything like us, you'll uncover other priorities—the kinds that generate financial opportunity *as a result of living true to what you're passionate about*—that are more central to your manifesto. Draw upon the work you've already done in the previous steps of the life-planning process to figure out what's important to you.

Your manifesto should capture your intentions and underlying principles and distill them into a simple statement—something you can carry in your wallet, memorialize in bold print on your desk, laminate and put on your wall, or type into your screen saver.

Once you crystallize your personal manifesto, you'll find that it affects the way you run your business and how people respond. In our case, for example, "work as family" is a guiding principle. When people come through our door, they immediately sense this. For most entrepreneurs, a formalized personal manifesto doesn't exist, but we've found that it's always easy to spot entrepreneurs whose businesses are driven by guiding principles. They're more focused in their work. Their marketing messages are clearer and more cohesive. Their priorities and principles shine through in what they do.

Step 6—Key Moves for the Life Plan

To make the most of your Life Plan, it has to be more than just illuminating—*you have to put it to work*.

To kick your Life Plan into high gear, it's imperative to

establish "key moves." This is where the rubber meets the road. This is where you transform your philosophy into strategy and tactics, where you transition from reflection to action. Your key moves will help you make your Life Plan a reality.

Figure out the steps you need to take to get from where you are today to where you want to be. Each of these key moves is essential—one depends on the other. Remember, achieving your business objectives is *not* your *ultimate* goal. Living the life you want *is*.

Go back to the example set by Joan Isabella of Yo! Radio. Before she became a mother, she was very involved in producing talk radio, and she was passionate about her work. The life-planning process helped her to decide that she wanted to work from home so she could have more time with her child. Joan's list of key moves looked something like this:

- Establish an independent radio consultancy
- Set up a home office with all the necessary audio and Internet capabilities
- Set a limit on the number of hours committed to work to make sure I have time for family
- Keep business opportunities flowing by staying in touch with my network of contacts

The Life Plan—Bringing It Together

Now that you've done all of the introspection, asked yourself some tough questions, dreamed up the lifestyle you'd like to lead, and prioritized what's important and what's not, you have the ingredients of your own Life Plan. Organize this info into a one- to two-page document. You can now use it to draw up a business plan that fits the life you want to lead.

Here's a sample of a Life Plan to give you a sense of what one looks like.

Sample Life Plan—2005

1. My Current Status
    a. Quality rating of my life on a scale of 1–100 (100 being best)
        ✓ 75
    b. My reality (responsibilities, level of funds, etc.)
        ✓ Responsible for ensuring my success, no kids, no pets, no mortgage
        ✓ Total annual expenses: $30,000
        ✓ Money available for year: $95,000
    c. Things that make me happy
        ✓ Doing something innovative and creative
        ✓ Getting lots of time with family
        ✓ Answering to no one but myself
        ✓ Working at home
    d. Things that make me unhappy
        ✓ Limited exposure to international travel
        ✓ No clear source of reliable income
        ✓ Not enough income
        ✓ No network of helpful contacts

2. My Ideal Life
        ✓ To fill every day with stimulating new challenges
        ✓ To have quality time with great friends and family members
        ✓ To create my own family
        ✓ To be my own boss

✓ To leave a legacy of achievement

✓ To travel the world with a purpose

✓ To make enough money to not worry about money

3. My Loves: What I Really Like Doing

✓ Teaching people new things

✓ Family time

✓ Playing piano

✓ Creating jewelry

4. My Skills & Capabilities: What I Do Well

✓ Public speaking

✓ Coming up with creative fashion designs

✓ Inspiring others to buy into my vision

✓ Written and oral communication

✓ Sensing opportunities in the market

5. My Track Record: What I Have Experience Doing

✓ Managing 10 employees at a jewelry company

✓ Managing financials

✓ Entering new fields and quickly learning the ropes

6. My Ideal Work Style

✓ Taking risks is okay—willing to "put it *all* on the line"

✓ Work at home

✓ Full-time

✓ Outsource as much as possible

✓ Don't want to manage a lot of people

7. My Manifesto

✓ Work is to be enjoyed, to be creative, and to support my lifestyle

8. My Key Moves to Get Me Where I Want to Be
- ✓ Keep a day job while setting up a home office for a part-time business
- ✓ Write a business plan for a full-time retail online jewelry business
- ✓ Start part-time but transition out of my job to work full-time from home

Our Bottom Line

Get in touch with your lifestyle needs and wants before you embark on launching a new business. Get your priorities in order. Get organized. Find out what really matters to you and what really makes you happy. Then set out to develop a business plan for a company that really fits the lifestyle of your dreams. Remember Antoine from the beginning of this chapter? Remember Kate from Birmingham? To ensure that you own your business instead of your business owning you, make your lifestyle the priority. Plan your life, *then* plan your business.

An Introduction

First, about "Super Startups." We've chosen five entrepreneurs and their companies to highlight how vast, varied, and fascinating the world of business has become. They've each been featured on our radio program as "Super Startup" stories. We transcribed dialogue from StartupNation Radio into the introductions for each of the Super Startups you'll find interspersed throughout the book.

In the lineup, you'll find everyone from working mothers to retirees—smart, savvy people just like you who are passionate about and devoted to their ideas. And while success is what these companies have achieved, you'll see that there's no single definition of success—it's different with each entrepreneur.

They range in size from Fresh Baby's two-sister team with $300,000 in estimated sales in 2004, to Cirrus Designs with 900 employees and $120 million in sales in 2004. All of them take advantage of technology and depend heavily on outsourcing functions like accounting and logistics, an important and growing trend in business these days.

Most important, they illustrate with color, humor, and passion the remarkable process of how an idea grows from virtually nothing into a full-fledged business.

All five entrepreneurs have had the same kind of "what if" epiphany that Jeff had on that rainy night almost two decades ago.

These entrepreneurs are typical of the kind of committed, passionate achievers who make up our fast-growing StartupNation community.

We'll introduce you to each of them and provide details of how they created their businesses, where they made mistakes, and how they moved on after stumbling over roadblocks. We'll show you how they've dealt with fast growth and success as well. Then, after each story, we'll summarize the key moves they've made.

Here's the first of those Super Startups: Gretchen Schauffler of Devine Color.

Home-Based Home Run

Devine Color, Inc.

Vital Stats

- Year Founded: 1999
- 2004 Revenue: $10 million in paint sales estimated
- No. of Employees: 4 (including founder Gretchen Schauffler and her husband, Scott David Goins)
- Headquarters: Port Oswego, Oregon
- For Radio Interview: www.startupnation.com/book

Big Idea

Create a 115-color paint line that makes it faster and simpler to choose paints for your home in colors that fit your personal taste, the natural features of your home (such as wood and stone), and even the part of the country you live in.

We first "met" Gretchen Schauffler on the airwaves in March 2004 when she was featured on StartupNation Radio. Here were the first words we exchanged on air:

SLOAN BROTHERS: *Let's go to Gretchen Schauffler—Gretchen, welcome to the show!*

GRETCHEN: *Thank you for having me!*

SLOAN BROTHERS: *Now, we wanted to make sure we understood some of your background, and you're described in some of the background material as a "petite powder keg."*

GRETCHEN: *Yes! I'm always laughing because how does a "nobody" who's not from the paint industry, who's not a designer, end up with a line that has revolutionized the paint industry?!*

We had the privilege of sitting down with Gretchen and her husband, Scott, at their home shortly after this radio interview. It was clear to us that Gretchen was living a carefully chosen lifestyle. She told us that working from home was a central part of her Life Plan. She particularly liked her commute, a short walk down the hall to her desk—the kitchen table.

Gretchen first began dabbling with color in 1994. She was a stay-at-home mom with two young daughters when she began to create artwork. She returned to her Puerto Rican roots for inspiration, creating collages featuring mirrors—"the cheap man's art," Gretchen calls it. "People really liked the pieces. They were funny and whimsical and really colorful. But what everyone mentioned was the way I made so many colors work together in these crazy collages," she remembers. Like any good entrepreneur, she started thinking about how she could sell the pieces beyond the several dozen that she had sold through galleries in the Portland area. She was looking into mass-producing them when Nordstrom's department store decided to feature a few of the collages in their gift guide in 1996. But mass-producing her very personal artwork couldn't be done, so Gretchen continued to paint and create.

Then she received a call from a woman asking if Gretchen could offer advice on how to paint a room. "She wanted to know if I could do for walls what I did in those pieces," she says. "I figured I might as well give it a try." One thing led to another and soon Gretchen had turned into a color consultant and was painting interiors in homes around Portland. Her first job paid $350. She was written up in the local newspaper *The Oregonian*. She got more and more business. "I became everybody's little secret. They loved the colors that I would hand-mix for them."

Then an old client called to ask her to do her whole house. Gretchen was getting so much business that she hired a painter to help out.

During this period, Gretchen received a call no business owner ever wants to take: a truly irate customer. "She said, 'Gretchen, you'd better get over here. This is horrible.' It was a disaster. The brown paint was awful. It clashed with the maple and walnut in her house, and the finish was like Vaseline. All greasy. The on-staff painter told her not to worry, that it would die down in about three months. That's like telling a woman with a terrible hair coloring job it will take 90 days to fix it."

As Gretchen told us her story, we could tell this day had been the *ah-hah!* day for her. It was the day when her ideas, her passion, her skills, and her creativity collided with awareness. Gretchen could see where the mistake had been made. The hired painter had used the color Gretchen had recommended but *not* Gretchen's preferred paint—it was a different manufacturer's brand. "It was then that I realized I needed my own paint line. I couldn't trust that my colors—what I envisioned for people's walls—would be perfect if I couldn't control which paint people were using. I couldn't trust the people who were mixing, tinting, and formulating paint."

The next day, Gretchen cracked open the Yellow Pages and started calling paint manufacturers. First on her list was Miller, a 110-year-old paint company. Gretchen jokes that she called them because they were within driving distance of her house. She also knew Miller had high-quality products, paint she could probably trust. The company, however, didn't have a high-end image. She thought maybe her ideas for paint, coupled with their manufacturing prowess, would spark some interest.

Miller turned her down flat. "They told me simply they couldn't see why they should mix somebody else's paint." Gretchen pushed a bit, she says, but it became really obvious that they weren't going to budge. Through a paint representative at a local store, she got the name of another paint manufacturer, who supplied paint to the mobile-home industry. "It wasn't high-quality paint. But he'd mix my colors for me, so I was in business," she says.

It was a smart move on Gretchen's part and a move that many entrepreneurs could learn from. Sometimes your first choice of a manufacturing partner isn't available. Many entrepreneurs trip up at this roadblock. They want a specific manufacturer, they want perfection the first time around, and they don't want to roll out a product that doesn't look and feel perfect. But perfection isn't something you should expect in the initial startup phase. Remember exactly what your priorities are. For Gretchen it was control: "I finally had control over the paint colors, and that's what I really needed."

The decision also gave her the opportunity to float her sense of color in front of consumers. She was in business.

Gretchen signed up three local paint stores to take the line. She hired a kitchen cabinet maker to build her a display more like something you'd see at a cosmetics counter than a paint store. She didn't have as many colors as the national brands, but she was convinced her colors were better. She made her labels by hand

and delivered paint to the stores herself. Then she got the idea of the "mini-pouch" when she and Scott brought home a bag of liquid margarita mix from Costco. "I didn't have the money to print up all those color chips. But I knew I needed to let people experience the colors in their homes." So she bought hundreds of Ziploc bags and, with the aid of her mother, grandmother, and her husband, Scott, she filled them up with enough of the Devine colors to paint several feet of a wall.

The samples were a huge hit. They sold 2,000 bags at $2 a piece in just three weeks in one store. They were so popular that once again *The Oregonian* got ahold of the story, writing in 2000 about how innovative Gretchen was in getting her business off the ground.

It was another pivotal moment for Gretchen, although at first she thought she'd really blown it. "I told the reporter that Miller had turned me down when I first asked them to make my paint. My statement was there in black and white. I had slammed Miller. So I called to apologize to the person who had first listened to my request. I thought it was all over. I'd never get Miller to make my paints. But the guy says, 'Actually, the new president of the company wants to see you.'"

The rest, as they say, is history. Gretchen stopped using the paint from her first manufacturer and signed a licensing deal with Miller that put her brand, her colors, and her recipe for a smooth, creamy, odorless paint in 450 stores by the end of 2004. And what's more, she was able to do it while staying true to her Life Plan. Not only was she in business, she was right at home—she found a way to establish national distribution while working from her kitchen table.

It's not hard to see how Gretchen became so successful. From behind our mikes at the StartupNation studio, we were completely wowed by this "petite powder keg" on the other end of the phone line. Everything we've learned about her approach to life and business rings true to the attributes of a classic entrepreneur. She's certainly got the energy and passion we look for.

There were several key moves she made in the creation of Devine Color that made her a success.

Gretchen's Key Moves:

1. **Focus.** Gretchen always stayed focused on her first "big idea": color. She's never wavered from believing that her core strength was how she saw the world's millions of hues and tones.

2. **Positioning and Innovation.** Gretchen positioned herself as an expert in color and design. She used that expertise and those skills in innovative ways to create products that made her very appealing to strategic partners and consumers. Just look at the mini pouches—they were a breakthrough way to inspire confidence in consumers and drive demand.

3. **She "Hitched Her Wagon to a Star,"** a practice we applaud. By teaming up with Miller Paint in a licensing and distribution agreement, she could focus on her core strengths—her divine sense of color and her ability to package and market it.

4. **Life Plan First.** Gretchen achieved all of this while staying true to her Life Plan. Her priority was to be at home and in proximity to her family. By making business decisions that were in sync with her ideal lifestyle, she now leads her dream life.

CHAPTER FOUR

Types of Businesses—What Fits You? What's Hot?

Pick a Business Model That's Right for You

So you've established the lifestyle you want to lead, the hours you want to work, your priorities, and your financial obligations. It's time to figure out how a business can fit into your life and facilitate the lifestyle you want to lead.

A PRIMER ON BUSINESS MODELS

While this is not intended to be an exhaustive list, here are some of the business models you might want to consider for your startup:

E-COMMERCE: An online retail business.

EBAY-PRENEURSHIP: An online marketplace that facilitates a web-based retail business. It's a relatively inexpensive way to start up and comes with a built-in marketplace. You can learn more about eBay-preneurship later in this section.

FRANCHISING: This model involves buying into a prepackaged business based on a proven formula. We also cover franchising in detail in the pages ahead.

(continued on next page)

HOME-BASED: This can be a full-time or part-time business operated from home. Over half of all small businesses are home-based today, and the numbers are rising. Women-owned businesses are the fastest-growing segment. Technology is playing a major role in making this possible.

BRICK AND MORTAR: Retail, manufacturing, professional services, and many other businesses that are located in various types of storefronts, buildings, and/or warehouses.

MULTILEVEL MARKETING: MLM is a marketing and distribution structure. People at the top sell to those below them, who in turn sell to those below them. The higher up you are in this structure, the more money you can make.

LICENSING: Ideal for inventors, this is an alternative to running a fully operational business. In licensing, you earn revenues from the company you've authorized to make, use, or sell your innovation. We go into detail on licensing later on.

As you can see, there's a world of possibilities when considering what business model might be best for you. Small businesses range from solo acts to companies with dozens of employees, from prime locations on Main Street to home-based offices like Gretchen Schauffler's, from a "high-touch" approach—with lots of direct customer interaction—to completely automated online operations. Some businesses must be full-time. Others can be conducted part-time, depending on the demands of the business and your lifestyle interests.

You may find that a hybrid strategy will work best for you. That was the case for Tom Nardone, an entrepreneur in his thirties who started out part-time—until he proved his business "had legs"—and then made the leap to full-time. He worked it out so he could take his company, ShopInPrivate.com, live during a two-week vacation from his full-time job.

We met Tom a few years ago and were immediately taken with

his business concept. ShopInPrivate.com sells everything you might be too embarrassed to buy at a drugstore. In 1998, Tom was working in the business-development office at Ford Motor Company, when he decided to try his hand at part-time entrepreneurship. Tom was driven by an almost biological need to strike out on his own. "My dad owned a liquor store in Wisconsin and my mom owned an ice cream store. I grew up with these two very entrepreneurial parents and knew how successful you could be being your own boss."

Tom happened upon the idea of ShopInPrivate.com while reading Robert McMath's book *What Were They Thinking*, which tells the stories of some of the best and worst product inventions in America. Tucked inside one of the chapters was a quick rundown of business niches the author thought were ripe for innovators to pursue. McMath wrote that if your idea eases other people's embarrassment, then you probably have a good idea for a business. "Now, if that paragraph doesn't have a business idea in it, I don't know what does," said Tom.

So while he was dreaming up new products for Ford, Tom sat down to sketch out a business plan. On the weekends, he researched the Internet, looking for competitors. He played around with Yahoo!'s website—building software to learn how to create a website without knowing any Internet computer language. He combed through wholesale magazines looking for products he thought people would be too embarrassed to buy from the clerk at their local drugstores. He picked items like nose hair clippers, adult diapers, Rogaine hair-growing gel, and hemorrhoid medications.

He incorporated his business on August 8, 1998, and put in a request for a two-week vacation in early October so he could launch the website without having to worry about interfering with his day job. "It was the best vacation I ever had. I typed up

QUICK TIP

One cautionary note—if you're considering starting a business related to your day job, make sure you check your employment agreement. Under some corporate guidelines, everything an employee creates, makes, or invents is the property of the employer. You also may have signed a noncompete agreement, which means if you decide to leave, you won't be able to take any of your favorite clients or customers with you. If you have any question about what you might be prohibited from doing, it's best to consult with an attorney.

press releases and sent them out to 400 newspapers and universities. I wrote about all the embarrassing things we'd sell on the site. On October 2, I sat for most of the day watching the website and waiting for the phone to ring. I made certain I could take online and phone-based orders. The phone didn't ring once. But in a couple of days the calls started to trickle in. By October 4, I had taken my first orders. I picked, packed, and shipped 10 orders that week. I was in business."

By the end of October, Tom was back at Ford while managing ShopInPrivate.com part-time. He pulled in $14,000 in orders that month. "People don't realize just how much you can get done on the weekends and the evenings. If you have e-mail, mobile phones, and voice mail, you can do this kind of business. Plus, you'd be surprised, but there are a lot of post offices that are open 24 hours if you need to get a package out fast."

Tom's business grew steadily. "It was great. I had this thriving little business that I did on the weekend and I still loved my job at Ford. There was no tightrope to walk. My livelihood didn't depend on whether the business sank or swam."

Today, Tom runs his online business full-time. He quit his job at Ford just six months after starting ShopInPrivate.com. Quitting wasn't in his original plan. He intended for ShopInPrivate to be a part-time endeavor. But Tom says the business started to take off in early 1999 as the dot-com boom really got going. "Valentine's Day 1999 was a really big turning point for us," Tom said, noting that their product lineup includes adult toys. The Valentine success was enough to prove to Tom that he actually didn't need his job at Ford. "But the great thing was I had proven the concept before I ever said good-bye to my day job."

Tom has morphed from part-time entrepreneur to full-time business owner with four full-time staffers, his own warehouse, and $2 million in annual revenues. He's a great example of a "pure e-tail" model.

Unlike Tom, maybe you're the type who'd prefer to dive right into a vertically integrated business with manufacturing, shipping, marketing, and more. Or maybe the idea of a low-fuss licensing model is more appealing. Like us, you could develop your business out of thin air. Or you could take the more predictable and preorganized path as a franchisee of a popular national business. Or maybe you're like one of those nearly half million people who've chosen "eBay-preneurship" as a business model. Whatever the type of business format, it can and should be molded to fit your Life Plan—not the other way around.

eBay-preneurship

If you still think eBay is only a place to auction off those Hummel figurines your grandmother gave you, think again.

In 2004, eBay estimated that more than 430,000 people—more people than work for corporate giants such as General Electric or Procter & Gamble—were making a living selling goods on eBay. The businesses range from part-timers such as Ann Whitley Wood, who sells high-end fashion items like Kate Spade bags and Lilly Pulitzer dresses that she finds at closeout sales, to MacNan Biologicals, a high school lab equipment business, generating $500,000 in revenue annually. MacNan was started by husband-and-wife team Mike and Nancy MacNamara after Mike was laid off from a large biological equipment supplier in 1995. eBay sales now account for more than 50 percent of their business.

"eBay did start off as a place for collectors to meet up with each other and for folks to sell the stuff they found in their attics," says Jay Fiore, senior manager for business marketing with eBay. "But it didn't take long for people to figure out that

The Fundamentals Still Apply

Make no mistake, an eBay business, like a business of any type, requires solid adherence to fundamentals in order to succeed.

It's crucial to distinguish your store from the competition on eBay. Your inventory and the way you present it must be very compelling. Stay focused on getting your goods packaged professionally and shipped on time. Otherwise, you'll damage your feedback rating and be at risk of losing repeat customers.

For more tips on how to do it right with an eBay store, check www.StartupNation.com/eBay. You can also find a great deal of useful information in Jim "Griff" Griffith's *The Official eBay Bible*. He's eBay's dean of education.

selling on eBay was a great secondary or even primary source of income." In fact, eBay has become one of the fastest and easiest ways to get your business started. With a small amount of inventory on hand, you can be in business within hours, participating in this huge online marketplace.

eBay is an option worth considering if you don't want to go to the expense or hassle of setting up your own retail website. "The fact is selling online can be difficult for small businesses. You have to worry about who's going to host the site, how you're going to deal with transactions, how you're going to take payments," Jay explains. "Once you're up and running, then you need to spend money on advertising to drive people to your website."

With eBay, all that's taken care of for you. Listing an item on eBay costs anywhere from 30 cents to $4.80, far cheaper than going through the cost of setting up your own e-commerce website and marketing your products outside of eBay. Receiving payment is facilitated by PayPal, an eBay subsidiary, which accepts most major credit cards.

But the biggest benefit is the sheer size and scope of eBay's marketplace. The site now draws about 135 million users in 28 countries. "There's just no way that a small-business owner could get that kind of traffic for their own site," Jay says. eBay has also become one of the most trusted places for people to shop online, with its feedback comments that help rate both buyers and sellers for quality of product and service.

eBay sees small businesses as a growing priority. Last year, it launched a series of workshops for business owners and has reserved rooms on its online community discussion boards for small-business owners to network with each other. Business purchasing has become a much larger part of eBay's business, with more and more businesses using the site to buy everything from office computers to industrial machines and tools. By 2003, Jay says, eBay estimated that more than $2 billion in business products were being sold on its site. "We had one customer who was in the process of opening his own pizzeria. He used eBay to buy everything he needed to start up his business, right down to the sign for his store. He figures he spent about $3,000 on used equipment that could've easily cost him $30,000 new."

eBay's a great way to get started in business, whether full-time or part-time. If you're passionate about having an online store, doing it the "eBay way" can make it easier.

Does Franchising Fit You?

Curves. The UPS Store. Sound familiar? They should. They're some of the country's most successful franchises. But deciding whether the franchising route is right for you and your Life Plan takes much more research than simply picking this year's hottest franchise and paying the fees.

Think of franchising as cutting off the "highs" and the "lows" of being an entrepreneur. You'll be giving up the thrill of starting a business based on your own idea, but you'll be more protected against failure. You'll still have to make a substantial up-front financial investment, and you'll have to be willing to work within strict franchising guidelines and requirements. But you'll be left with a proven formula for you to execute effectively, with the franchisor standing behind you to support you each step along the way.

With that in mind, here are a few questions to ask yourself about whether franchising is right for you.

FAST FACTS: FRANCHISING

- Franchising accounts for 10 percent of the U.S. gross national product
- Franchises generate 40 percent of U.S. retail sales
- Franchising brings in $1.5 trillion in annual revenues
- Franchises are active in more than 75 different industries, including law firms, hotels, and medical practices

Source: iFranchise Group

---

1. Do you want "a sure thing"? As Mark Siebert, chief executive officer of iFranchise Group, says, "Franchises are about replicating success, not creating success." If you're the type of person who wants to see your name on the door and the praise and perks of running your own show, you should think twice about buying into a franchise.

2. Do you have responsibilities that make striking out on your own impossible? If you have a family or other responsibilities, franchising can be a viable option. As a franchisee, you can expect to keep regular hours after the first few months of startup. You can hire salespeople to run the store, and you may even receive help in hiring and training people from your franchisor. Keep in mind, however, that franchising can be expensive, especially in the first year when you're building the business and not raking in big profits. If you have financial responsibilities, make sure you have the capital to see you through at least a year of running the franchise.

3. Are you better at "doing" than "creating"? If you like running the operations of a business, franchising may be perfect for you. You buy into a franchise for the formula. If you choose a high-quality franchise and follow the prescribed formula, you're likely to become a success. However, if you're

the creative type, be careful what kind of franchise you choose. Many franchisors keep tight control over what happens with their franchisees. A franchisor is fully within their rights to sue if you don't follow their rules.

If you decide that franchising is for you, the most important thing you can do is research the possibilities—there's a broad variety of franchising options available. Try to focus on franchises that are in a niche you're familiar with and passionate about. Here are some crucial factors you should think about in order to make a good choice:

• **A firsthand feel.** There's nothing more valuable than personally experiencing the service and products of the franchise. So visit a location of the franchise you're considering. Or visit two or three. Gauge the overall experience. And don't be shy about talking to other customers to get their impressions. If you like what you learn, it's a good sign. Trust your instincts.

• **Number of locations in your community.** Check the number of franchise locations that already exist in your vicinity. Some franchisors use franchisees to grow very rapidly, saturating the market and making it difficult for latecomers to make a profit. To check on whether you're likely to face slow crowds and low profits, every month or so check in on existing locations of the franchise you're targeting to see how busy they are.

If the franchisor is new and you'd be the first to introduce the concept to your area, this can present opportunity and risk. On the risk side, the franchise concept will be unproven in your area. You won't know how much demand to expect. On the opportunity side, you might be able to negotiate a territory exclusive with the franchisor if you're one of the first to sign up.

- **Look-alikes.** Assess how easy it would be to copy the franchise concept you're considering. Check for knockoffs that are popping up in the form of competitive franchises and independent businesses. Perhaps you can find a franchise business concept that has a high barrier to entry for competitors, such as a proprietary recipe or a patented product. You don't want to buy into a franchise that's likely to turn into a commodity business.

- **Make a visit to the franchise headquarters.** This is an effective way to figure out if the franchise is a good fit for you and if you're a good fit for the franchise. Do you like the people in management? Are the founders still working at least part-time in the business? Do they make you feel like a part of the team? These are just some of the questions you should ask yourself before you make the franchise leap.

Once you've decided on what franchise you're interested in, begin researching the financial commitments you'll have to meet. According to the International Franchise Association, the average initial investment to open a franchise location is less than $250,000. Take into account the startup fee you'll have to pay to the franchisor—on average, around $25,000. It's just the first of many fees you'll pay over the years to run the franchise.

Meet the Brady Bunch

"A lot of franchisees want the best of both worlds. That is, they want the freedom of doing whatever they please with their business, but they also want the added safety of using a tried and true business model," says Dan Brady, part of a family that owns seven UPS Store franchise locations in the Philadelphia area.

According to Stuart Mathis, president of Mail Boxes Etc. ("The UPS Store"), the Bradys—Al the father (68), Steve the second born (42), Kevin the third born (41), Dan the fourth born (37), and Jeanne the fifth born (34)—are referred to as "The Brady Bunch." In 1999, they were awarded Mail Boxes Etc. Franchisee of the Year. They earned approximately $3.1 million in revenue in 2004, with a plan to double that number in the near term. They're a shining example of entrepreneurs who've made a success buying and operating a franchise.

But that wasn't always the case. In 1989, Mail Boxes Etc. was still an independent company (one that UPS would acquire in April, 2001, and re-brand "The UPS Store"). That was the year the Bradys decided to get into business for themselves. Their inspiration to run their own business came at a time when Steve, number-two son, was searching for a new career. He wanted to find something with more potential than the delivery route he was driving for Frito Lay. Al supported his son's desire to find a better opportunity, and he was willing to leave his career working as an executive at a big corporation to follow through on his paternal instincts. After a lot of discussion about what type of business to go into and which business model best suited their personal capabilities, resources, and objectives, the Bradys decided on franchising. They believed that buying a franchise would be less risky than starting up a new business, and that suited the new entrepreneurs just fine.

After exhaustively researching the franchise options, they settled on Mail Boxes Etc.—then a hot concept with locations mostly in the western United States, and growing very quickly. The Bradys recall that there were only a couple hundred Mail Boxes Etc. on the east coast at the time, so they felt they'd have a shot at getting in on the ground floor in Philadelphia.

Once they settled on the franchisor, they struck a deal with

Mail Boxes Etc. to open a store in Frazer, a suburb of Philadelphia. They took the bold steps that entrepreneurs are well known for—Al and Steve left their jobs. Al provided $100,000 of his savings to finance the initial location. Al would oversee Steve, and Steve would run the store. It was a huge personal commitment they were making, but the Bradys were filled with optimism about their new store and the opportunity it represented. Little did they know, their optimism would quickly give way to a tough dose of reality.

The first sign of trouble was low customer traffic. They had located the store in a strip mall. But the mall was very large and there was poor visibility from the road. The old adage, "Out of sight, out of mind" was becoming part of their new reality. Further, the suburb they had chosen was still very underdeveloped. It didn't provide the population density that would become central to their future formula for success. They found themselves fighting an uphill battle in a business that struggled for three years with anemic sales and no profit in sight.

Representatives from Mail Boxes Etc. approached the Bradys with a possible solution. They recommended that the Bradys buy out an existing franchise. The store they had in mind was based in Lionville, another suburb of Philadelphia. It was being run by an older couple who—because they were nearing retirement—weren't giving the business as much attention as it deserved. The thought was that with the Bradys' energy and ambition, they could purchase the franchise and infuse it with new life to make it perform at full potential.

While Steve tried to make a go of the original store, Kevin, third oldest, returned home to run the Lionville location. Unlike Steve, Kevin had retail experience—he'd been managing a lumber yard in upstate New York for several years. Kevin became general manager of the new store and things immediately took off—store

#2 was a hit. They quickly realized that the battles they'd fought to make the first location work were unique to that location. Just 12 months later, the Bradys bit the bullet on the original location and closed up shop. They lost $100,000.

It was a tough lesson and it reinforced the popular business wisdom that location makes all the difference. Had they located their first store better with more visibility and greater population density, the story might have been different. It certainly was at store #2.

"Store #2 turned out to be a very good move. Our franchisor was supporting us. They wanted us to succeed and were proactive in helping us find a good location. Our major breakthrough, though, was learning that sometimes it's better to buy out an existing location rather than start a brand-new one. We try to find franchisees who've already proven that the location works. Buy them out and bring in your energy, and you can grow a mediocre store into a profitable one much quicker than if you started a brand-new location. Of our seven stores, the ones that we purchased from other franchisees return the invested dollar much quicker."

The Bradys had an appetite to develop more than two stores and would need a capable team to grow new locations. They didn't have to search far. Fresh out of law school in 1995, Dan was the fourth Brady to enter the business, just months after the Bradys identified yet another location owned by a franchisee who was ready to sell out.

The Bradys pressed on, growing their group of franchise locations. While the next few years in business were marked mostly by perfecting their formula, there was one major surprising event. UPS decided to acquire Mail Boxes Etc. But, fortunately for the Bradys, the creation of the new brand—The UPS Store—brought them nothing but more opportunity. Dan recalls, "When The

UPS Store sign was hung outside our front doors, we saw a significant increase in package count and revenue—and that was especially true for lower-performing stores across the Mail Boxes Etc. system."

After 15 years, seven franchise locations, and millions in revenue, listen to what the Brady Bunch has to say about being a successful franchisee:

1. Learn as much as you can about the franchisor—who started it, who's operating it. Look into their history. Determine their performance.
2. Get ahold of the FOC (see Quick Tip) and read it word for word. Make sure you understand and are comfortable with all the major provisions of the contract. Be clear on what you're giving up and what you're getting.
3. Secure your financing and make sure you work operating capital into your thinking. Get a minimum of 8 to 12 months of operating capital over and above startup funds. Build in a 20 percent or so cushion of financing over and above what your franchisor suggests you'll need.
4. Spend a lot of time on building a rock-solid business plan. If you don't have any experience with this, find some experts who do. It's not just for financiers—it's something you'll use as a living document. There's no difference in the importance of a business plan whether it's for a franchise business or a nonfranchise business. You can't rely solely on the franchisor to provide you with a turnkey business plan that fits your particular business opportunity. That has to come from you.
5. Lock up your geographic area. A good franchisor will help you understand what the right density is for stores in your territory.
6. Location. Location. Location. It really holds true. No matter how good an operator you are, it comes down to having that

business in the right location. We look at household income, traffic flows, daytime population, and real estate that's affordable, accessible, and appealing.

7. Stick with one location if you're an individual or a husband-and-wife team and want to keep it simple. Go the route of multiple locations if you want to make more money and you don't mind building up and managing the infrastructure necessary to make this work. Keep in mind that some day you may desire to sell your business. When that happens, note that individual locations sold as part of a group of locations generally are worth more than those sold as stand-alone locations.

8. We've never opened two at a time—it causes too much financial and operational strain. The biggest challenge we felt was when we grew from two to three locations, not from one to two. We didn't have an organization set up to handle multiple locations. While franchisors do a great job setting you up to open and run a single location, they often don't offer a lot of value when setting up multiple locations.

9. Try to get involved in your franchisor's national committees. Dan says that his dad sits on The UPS Store Multiple Center Owner Committee, formed in 2003. The rest of the Bradys are very involved in other national committees at The UPS Store, including the Marketing Advisory Council, the Profit Action Committee, and the Technology Committee.

Licensing Your Great Idea

One of the most streamlined business models—one that's particularly appropriate for commercializing inventions—is licensing. You don't need to have any infrastructure, you don't need to hire people, and you assume only minimal financial risk. Licensing is a type of transaction in which you grant a company the right to make, use, and/or sell your product or invention. In return, you receive payment in the form of a "royalty." The company to whom you grant the rights is known as the "licensee," and you're the "licensor." The licensee takes all the risk of producing and marketing the product, and in exchange keeps the lion's share of the net sales proceeds, paying you an average royalty amount of typically 5 to 10 percent. If it works, it can be a big win for both parties.

If you want to go the licensing route, you'll likely need to have a pending patent—or better yet, an *issued* patent—in order to get a company's serious consideration. You should have a prototype, production-cost estimates, and market-research data that demonstrates there will be demand for the product in the marketplace. Next, you'll begin identifying and making contact with potential licensees.

Some big companies will consider unsolicited submissions, but many will not. To identify the potential licensees, find companies that already produce and sell similar or complementary products. Contact each of these companies to determine the appropriate procedures for submission. Our advice is to research multiple companies in the industry you're targeting for your invention. Study company websites. Read through press releases and new-product announcements. Pay special attention to companies that highlight their licensing agreements with outsiders.

For example, Dial Corporation positions itself publicly as a licensing-friendly company that supports innovators. That shows a real willingness to consider outside submissions. And don't forget, when you start the dialogue, pay careful attention to the confidentiality policies practiced by each company.

Drawing on our experience in licensing—which started with the Battery Buddy and led to a business dedicated to helping others license their inventions—we've compiled a list of lessons that, when adhered to, can help you avoid the pitfalls that trip up many inventors:

- If your idea isn't patented, you should try to get a confidentiality agreement (also referred to as a "nondisclosure agreement") signed before submitting your proprietary information to anybody or any company. The challenge is that many companies won't sign the agreement as a matter of procedure. If this happens, provide just enough information about your product or idea to get them interested in learning more. Once they're curious, require them to sign a confidentiality agreement in order to learn more.

- If your idea's already patented and in the public domain, you might try enlisting someone within the company who could become an advocate for your invention. Having someone on the inside who believes in your product and who'll make sure you're getting the attention you deserve can reduce months of process into weeks of action and can get you to a "Yes" or "No" rapidly.

- Saying "Yes" to taking on new products is always risky for decision makers at big companies. For them, it's much easier and safer to say "No." To make them feel more comfortable about saying yes, anticipate and address every concern they may raise. The more real-world data and research you can provide, the easier it'll be for them to ultimately say "Yes."

- Dealing with the common "not invented here" syndrome at big companies is tricky. Many product developers and engineers at big companies believe they know best. If the idea isn't theirs, many times it's discounted as not worthy or not valuable to the company. Overcome this mindset by encouraging them to enhance or improve upon your idea so they feel like it's their own. You might be able to transform "not invented here" into "must have here."

• If you're fortunate enough to be offered a license agreement, always use an attorney experienced specifically in licensing to negotiate and finalize the deal. There are many ways to structure these agreements, and in most cases, you only get one shot, so don't cut corners here.

For example, you'll have to decide whether you want an exclusive or nonexclusive license agreement. If you choose an exclusive license, the downside is that you'll be prohibited from selling the invention to anyone else. But the upside is that exclusive licenses frequently command a higher royalty *as well as* an up-front, lump-sum payment from the licensee.

If you choose a nonexclusive licensing agreement, you'll be able to pursue multiple licensing relationships. When we were licensing the Battery Buddy, we opted for an exclusive agreement with Masco Industries, which prohibited us from licensing the invention directly to the automakers, like GM and Ford. If you believe your invention has several distinct markets, and you'd be better served by pursuing a variety of licensees, hold out for a nonexclusive agreement. But keep in mind that you may not be able to negotiate either an advance or a minimum royalty in a nonexclusive agreement.

You'll also be glad you have a seasoned attorney on your side when it comes time to negotiate your royalties. In general, "net" royalties are calculated against the gross price of the product minus shipping, insurance, taxes, and an allowance for returns. But "net" is a subjective term, so defining it is crucial. You may have to agree to a marketing allowance, usually not more than 5 percent. The licensee may also want to amortize the capital costs of tooling if your invention has to be manufactured. Just be sure you don't let the licensee include general costs of doing business, such as salaries or rent, in their calculation of net royalties. And *never* let them talk you into a royalty arrangement where they have to make a profit *before* you get your money. You'll end up never getting paid.

• Before you close a licensing agreement, make sure you require the licensee to present their plan for marketing your product so you can have confidence they're taking the opportunity seriously. Once you sign the license agreement, it's out of your hands, so confirm in advance that they're devoting the necessary resources to making your product a success.

• Never let your rights be held hostage by a company. Always negotiate a "minimum annual royalty" payment, the minimum amount the licensee must pay you even if they don't sell a single unit. With this requirement, they either pay this amount or lose their exclusive rights to the product. Regardless of how well the licensee performs, with a minimum annual royalty requirement, you can be assured of receiving a baseline amount of royalties.

"What's Hot?"

As we travel the country giving seminars and broadcasting our StartupNation Radio show, one of the most common questions we're asked is "What's Hot?" But if you're looking to create a successful business, a better question to ask is "What *makes* a business hot?"

While it's true that, at any given time, there are "hot" businesses in the marketplace, it's better to focus on the key ingredients that make those businesses perform so well. Understand those ingredients and you're on your way to designing a business that's *hot*!

To begin, drop your preconceived notions about having to come up with *"the next big thing."* We've concluded that there

> **QUICK TIP**
>
> Be careful about being taken in by invention brokerage services that require you to pay a large fee up front for nothing more than evaluating your invention and placing it on their list of licensable products. While there are legitimate brokerage services out there, make sure you check their track record before you do business with any one of them. Otherwise, you might end up wasting a lot of money and precious time while your invention sits idly on a list with thousands of other neglected inventions.
>
> Truth is, many of these brokers make money from up-front fees paid by naive inventors, and are rarely successful in licensing an invention.

are a far greater number of successful businesses out there that are *not* revolutionary at all—instead, they're *evolutionary*. They're distinguished by their subtle but game-changing improvements over existing products and services. In some cases, they're distinguished by a shift in the way the business is executed. For example, it might be creating better operational efficiencies, new channels of distribution, or new ways of marketing.

Look no further than Method Products, started in 2000 and now generating over $40 million in annual sales. What do they sell? Soap. That's right, soap—the stuff that's been a commodity product for decades. You can conjure up the major brands almost instantaneously: Dial, Dove, Safeguard, and the list goes on. So how is it that Method's young founders, Adam Lowry and Eric Ryan, have been able to build such a hot business in the midst of these entrenched brands?

They started by taking a fresh look at the category. They concluded that the products were "tired." To carve out a niche, they decided to create a new line of soaps, but to make them using non-toxic ingredients. They also created ergonomic dispensers that actually looked hip next to your sink rather than being an eyesore. From there it was all marketing and making key distribution relationships. Many of the trendy home and lifestyle magazines picked up on their press releases, and they even got the product "placed" on the NBC hit show *Friends*. Translating this exposure into consumer demand, they've been able to get their products onto more than 8,000 "shelves"—the industry term for retailer space where their product is sold—including those of Target and Costco.

Adam and Eric's success story demonstrates that the "next big thing" could be as simple as a slight improvement on a bar of soap or any other product or service that's been around for a long time.

Speaking of products that have been around a long time, what about swords? Think they're a thing of the past? Titus Blair doesn't. He started a company called SwordsOnline.com in January 1998, with $550 cash. He was 22 at the time and decided to start up a company that was a natural outgrowth of his combined interest in the Internet and swords.

When we first met Titus, we asked him, "How big a business could this possibly be?" He was quick to let us know. "There's been a wave of movies in recent years where the main characters use swords—*Gladiator, Lord of the Rings*, and *The Last Samurai* are examples—and I rode the wave of that exposure," said Titus. During this same period, eBay began stirring up broad interest in collecting. When you combine the two phenomena and start doing the math, you begin to realize just how big Titus Blair's hobby opportunity could become. The fact is, Titus's business has grown at an astonishing rate and SwordsOnline.com has become the world's leading e-tailer of swords. He's expanded his product line to include thousands of collectible weapons, and his 2004 revenue was approximately $3.25 million.

In addition to the key lessons you can learn from the success of SwordsOnline.com and Method Products, here are some other essentials that make a business hot:

- **Address a Screaming Need.** When the market is asking for something and you can provide it, that's called "addressing a screaming need." Businesses like the eBay packaging and shipping stores address a screaming need. Mobile lunch vans that visit job sites during the midday work break address a screaming need. Educational businesses that help people pass their certification exams, like LSATs or real estate license exams, address a screaming need.

  It's always easier to market something that people already want than it is to convince them that they should want what you are marketing. If you do have to convince customers about the value of what you're selling, the costs of marketing will be higher and customer adoption will be slower.

- **Find a Niche and Fill It.** Focusing on filling a niche will allow you to target your resources and establish success in one market before you try to enter other markets and risk spreading yourself too thin. A perfect example is what Stephanie Odegard did with her company. Having identified an underserved need for higher quality hand-made rugs that could be sold at a premium price point, she founded Odegard Carpets, Inc., which she based in a small Manhattan office. Stephanie created original designs, arranged to have them hand-made by the finest artisans in Nepal, and focused her initial marketing dollars directly on creating awareness in the premium rug niche.

  Her decision to focus paid off in spades. Today, Stephanie runs a business with operations on three continents employing thousands of people. Odegard carpets are found in many prestigious locations around the world including the Getty Museum in Los Angeles, Robert Redford's home, and the Chambers Hotel in New York, to name a few. She was able to establish her company as the premier brand in her niche, and now she is branching out in new markets with new products, such as high-end furniture. She successfully found a niche, filled it, and then built on her brand strength and track record to launch new lines.

- **Streamline Your Operations.** If you want to be successful, you should keep your operations lean and mean. To learn how to streamline, look no further than Dell. They have more market share than any other computer company—over 18 percent of the worldwide PC market as of late 2004. They currently produce nearly 100,000 computers a day to meet the demand. The amazing part is that Dell has created a business model that has no factories, no warehouses, no trucks, and no stored inventory. Dell is the master of innovative techniques that streamline operations and keep costs low. Because they do this so well, Dell hammers the competition by delivering the best product at the best price with the best profit margins. Dell sells over the Internet, which cuts out expensive retail store operations. Dell has no financing outlays for producing inventory—instead, you, their customer, finance the *just-in-time* production of each computer. In most cases, Dell has negotiated to pay its suppliers on 30-day terms. Once your computer is built, it's immediately shipped out to you right from the factory, thus avoiding expensive warehousing. All of these principles can be applied to the operations of your business. Whether you're thinking of an online business or a specialty candy store in your hometown, learn from the Dell model the many techniques that will help you keep your inventory moving, negotiate favorable terms with suppliers to help manage cash flow, and keep facility and personnel burdens to a minimum by outsourcing non-core activities.

- **Leverage Technology.** Create a website, update your cell phone functionality, and purchase software to run your business more efficiently. These three moves alone could transform your business. When you leverage technology, you free up time—perhaps your most precious resource. Leveraging technology also reduces your operating costs so you can spend your funds on marketing and other strategic budget items. Technology also enables you to connect with and understand your customers like never before.

To drive traffic to his online store, Titus Blair of Swords-Online.com used the power of search-engine advertising to buy prime placement on search sites like Google. He also used search engines to optimize the content and construction of his site so searches conducted on the Internet would pull up SwordsOnline.com first.

Titus also automated as many of his business functions as possible. He uses tracking software on his site to learn from his customers' usage patterns as they shop. This helps him know the specific interests of his customers and helps guide him when making marketing and inventory decisions.

If your business is currently brick and mortar, consider equipping your company with e-commerce capability. U.S. online retail sales will more than double over the next five years, reaching $316 billion by 2010.

The benefit of technology is even more pronounced for a pure e-tail business. Because sales are transacted much more efficiently online, profit margins for e-tailers have surged to 21 percent, whereas profit margins for brick-and-mortar stores are traditionally in the range of 3 to 10 percent.*

- **Kick Up Your Customer Service.** To illustrate how customer service can make your startup red hot, let's go right back to Mike Palmer, whom we introduced to you in Chapter One. Mike's business has become more profitable each year even though his store, Premier Pet Supply, is surrounded by 14 national-chain pet-supply retailers. How does he do this? Supreme customer service, which we cover in further detail in Chapter Seven.

- **Be the Expert.** If you want to leap to the top of the list when people think about your kind of product or service, make yourself *the* authority. The credibility that comes from this kind of status and positioning is priceless. When you're an expert, people will have confidence in what you offer. They'll be more accepting of your product or service and the price you charge.

    Scott Griggs knows this to be true. He makes millions of dollars each year selling model trains through his online business, Trainz.com. He's one of the top sellers on all of eBay and is *the* top seller in the toy and hobby category.

---

*Retail sales and profit margins reported by shop.org and Forrester Research in 2004 in their annual survey of retailers.

What leads to this kind of stratospheric success on eBay? Scott says, "You must specialize in something. You must have intimate knowledge of what you're selling and be a bona fide expert in that product line." Scott has established a reputation among collectors of model trains. When hobby stores or individuals who have major collections want to sell all or a portion of their inventory, they go right to Scott.

- **Monitor the Trends.** Up until now, we've been focusing on ingredients that make a business hot. But if you're the type that's not content with merely improving upon an existing business idea and are determined to discover the *"next big thing,"* one way to begin is to start watching social trends. Identifying trends and linking them with commercial opportunities is possible if you train yourself to be keenly aware.

Look around. Consider your everyday life. Get tuned in. Which chores—which processes—in your daily routine have room for improvement? Which products are missing that, if you had them, would make things easier for you? For example, if you'd noticed there should be an easier way to send out items to people who bought from your eBay site, you might have anticipated the idea of an eBay drop-off service such as those that are now popping up everywhere.

You should also look beyond your personal experience-- listen to your friends, family members, and colleagues at work. What are they talking about? What's working for them and what's not? What services and products would they like to add to their daily routine to make their lives easier?

Become a media maven. Scour newspapers and magazines, tune in to talk radio to hear the concerns and opinions of the masses, spend time in chat rooms on the Internet, and watch TV—that's right, TV. And don't skip the commercials. Look for cultural shifts, changing demographics, emerging technologies, and consumer buying patterns. Look for ways you can turn these macro trends in the marketplace into business opportunities.

Take a look at some of the trends we've noticed recently and the new opportunities they're spawning:

Market Trend 1—The Graying of America. According to the 2002 U.S. Census, 16 percent of our population is now 60 years old or older, and they represent nearly 45 million Americans. Business opportunities to address their special needs are abundant. For example, tens of millions of senior Americans require in-home care and this number will only grow. Who will fill this need and how will they do it?

Market Trend 2—Women and Hispanics are examples of population segments that have ever-increasing buying power. According to Delia Passi, founder of Medelia Communications and former group publisher of *Working Woman* and *Working Mother* magazines, women are responsible for over 85 percent of all consumer purchases. Understanding the unique products they seek and how to market to them presents numerous opportunities. Hispanic purchasing power is expected to hit $1.2 trillion in 2010 according to the Hispanic Marketing and Communication Association. Many specialty advertising companies and consultants are already profiting by assisting corporations in understanding how to specifically address this market. Who will fill this need and how will they do it?

Market Trend 3—Mind, Body, Soul. There's a growing interest in products and services that address America's desire to be more healthy and more spiritual. We've witnessed the mainstreaming of yoga studios over the last few years, and now we're seeing massage and even acupuncture going mainstream through a variety of franchises. And organic foods continue to grow in popularity. Now there's even a category in stores called "local foods" that have the appeal of being more fresh due to their local origins and "functional foods" that are not only satisfying but good for you. A good example would be the new bottled waters with vitamins and minerals in them. What other products or services will cater to this growing trend? And who will fill this need and how will they do it?

Market Trend 4—Mentoring. There's a growing demand for people to have access to a mentor to help with all kinds of life's challenges. A whole new industry has emerged based on providing the service of "coaching" to assist people in reaching personal and professional goals. This includes business coaching, fitness training, and general life coaching. The demand is surging and the efficiencies of the telephone and Internet are allowing a great deal of the interaction to take place from home. Can you fill this need?

Market Trend 5—Disintermediation. This trend results from using the Internet as a way to cut out the middleman and connect people directly to each other. eBay does it in the auction world by connecting buyers and sellers; Match.com does it in the matchmaking world by connecting singles; and now we're seeing it happen in the real estate business. By posting a home for sale on the Internet on one of the many "for sale by owner" sites, and by paying directly for services to help facilitate the showing of the property and the sale, sellers are able to cut out the hefty traditional commission costs.

> **QUICK TIP**
>
> The more trends you can respond to with one business idea, the hotter your business will be. Take the women's 30-minute fitness franchise phenomenon "Curves" with over 8,000 franchise locations. It appeals to the need to be efficient with time AND the desire to be fit—each of which are two major trends today.

Our Bottom Line

If you can identify a trend or find a niche for a business and a way to leverage technology, you're going to be hot. If you can find a niche, leverage technology, and kick up your customer service, you're going to be hot. If you can find a niche, leverage technology, kick up your customer service, become "the" expert, and streamline operations, you're going to be *very* hot. And, if you can do all of this *and* address a screaming need in the market, you're going to be *on fire!*

SUPER STARTUP #2

From Inspiration to Patent to Profit

SkyDeck Industries, LLC

Vital Stats

- Year Founded: 2002
- 2004 Revenue: $2.4 million in licensing and royalty fees
- No. of Employees: 5
- Founders: Jim Teeter and Frank Messano
- Headquarters: Lake Arrowhead, California
- For Radio Interview: www.startupnation.com/book

Big Idea

Reinvent the RV experience by reengineering the roof of the vehicle to become an outdoor living room.

We first "met" Frank Messano on the airwaves in January 2004 on StartupNation Radio. Here are the first words we exchanged with Frank:

SLOAN BROTHERS: We're talking with Frank Messano from Sky-Deck Industries. Frank, welcome to the show!

FRANK: Thank you for having me!

SLOAN BROTHERS: Listeners, picture yourself going down the highway in the RV. You get to your destination . . . maybe it's a little crowded, you kind of want to get above it all. . . . What are people going to do? Frank?

FRANK: They're going to go up the interior stairway, like in a home, open the hatch on top, seats will automatically unfold, there'll be a series of sofas, a barbecue, a wet bar . . .

SLOAN BROTHERS: Unbelievable!

FRANK: No, it's believable!

SLOAN BROTHERS: Well, what about the hot tub?

FRANK: Actually, that's coming down the line, it's part of the original patents!

We love the story of how Frank Messano came up with his idea for an invention that has revitalized the RV industry.

Messano and his wife were traveling in their RV in the Northwest one day when they decided to park along the beach. They were hoping for a nice view but they didn't get it. Parked behind a bunch of other RVs in the crowded campground, they couldn't see the ocean or the beach. It was just by chance that Frank decided to go up on the roof, where their outdoor chairs were stowed. "It was just so neat up there," said Frank. "It was quiet and I could see out to the ocean. It was like being on the flying bridge of a boat. I came back down about four hours later."

Frank's story is the perfect example of how inspiration for an idea can come from anywhere—even on the top of an RV in a crowded campground. It's the kind of story we think everyone can relate to. Who hasn't thought to themselves "Hey, why didn't I think of that?"

But it took Frank four years to take that rooftop inspiration and turn it into the SkyDeck, a patented system that includes motorized handrails, a whirlpool, barbecue, and seating for more than 10 people, depending on the size of the RV. To "get real," Frank took on and completed the rigorous, time-consuming patent process all by himself. He built his own prototype from his old RV and endured rejection from industry executives who would eventually end up waiting in lines at trade shows just for the chance to stand on Frank's SkyDeck.

Frank's first stop on the trip to "getting real" about his idea was the patent office. As an industrial designer for decades, Frank was well aware of how the patent process works. Unlike most inventors, he was uniquely equipped to file his patent without the assistance of a professional (which is what we normally recommend). "The patent office, I find, treats you much better if you're doing it yourself. They bent over backwards to help me."

For two years, Frank worked through the patent process with a patent examiner at the U.S. Patent and Trademark Office. At one point, the examiner found something remarkably similar to the Sky-Deck that was invented at the turn of the twentieth century, showing a "wheeled horse-drawn cart with a roof deck." "That's how thorough they are at the patent office," Frank warns. But he didn't wait around for the patent to be issued. He started tearing apart his RV to build a prototype. He also began thinking about how he was going to approach the RV industry to commercialize his invention. "There's so little focus on research and development in the industry. They're very stuck in their ways—business as usual."

That makes it very easy for RV companies to say no to any new inventions. So Frank did his best to counteract their potential objections to licensing the SkyDeck before he approached them for the first time. Unlike many licensors, he decided to pay for the tooling and molds himself, anticipating that the RV companies would say no to something that would be a significant cost for them.

In 2002, with his patent near completion (his claims had all been allowed), he began sending out photos, drawings, and proposals to the biggest RV manufacturers. "I didn't hear one word back from most of them. Others had their secretaries send me form letters telling me this was unsolicited information. I decided it just wasn't a fit for the industry."

So Frank tried a different tactic. He made a nice-looking prototype and took it to an RV "aftermarket" show, a show for accessories that are produced and installed after the time of manufacture. The SkyDeck was a huge success. "People were lined up by the thousands," Frank says. But the biggest boon to Frank's business was meeting Jim Teeter, who worked at a company that owned a national network of RV dealerships. Teeter was "a young fellow with a sterling reputation for honesty in the RV business," Frank says. "I talked to him about SkyDeck, and he finally said to me 'I want to be a part of this.'"

Two weeks later, Jim got Frank interviews with two of the biggest RV manufacturers in the country, Thor America and Airstream, both owned by Thor Industries. "We got agreements on the spot to license SkyDeck," Frank said. With the agreement signed, Frank thought that was the end of his involvement. Thor and Airstream would take the tooling and machinery and start making prototypes of the SkyDeck to take to their dealer shows. He was ready to move on to several more ideas and patents that he thought would be as revolutionary as SkyDeck. "But Jim had other ideas. He told me we had to choreograph those dealer shows. He knew all too well that the RV manufacturers' salespeople wouldn't know how to sell it. He showed up with two well-trained salespeople. We set records that day with 130 orders."

For Frank it was an eye-opening experience. "Any good idea has to be sold. If you can't sell it, it's just a dream."

Today, Frank and his partner, Jim, are moving ahead with several more ideas for the RV industry, including a vehicle that's reminiscent of something you'd see in a James Bond movie. As this book goes to press, Frank is close to getting a patent for a combination RV/boat.

Frank's Key Moves

It's hard to know where to start with Frank's key moves, because he did so many things right. But here are a few of the most important ones:

1. **Protect Through Patents.** He knew exactly where to go first—the patent office. He started protecting his idea early on. That's a smart move, given that unscrupulous people won't hesitate to steal a good idea. It's also smart because potential licensees will attribute much greater value to your invention if they can commercialize it knowing it's patented.

2. **Market Research.** Frank thoroughly investigated the industry that would be interested in his product. He understood what their objections would be before he approached them. That kind of up-front research can save you a lot of time and effort, and significantly enhances your odds of success.

3. **Reducing Risks.** Finally, Frank bit the bullet by building molds and tooling himself so the RV makers wouldn't push back based on cost fears. He also generated immense market interest by building a prototype and taking it to trade shows. By the time he got into serious dialogue with the RV makers, he had a *business opportunity* for them, not just a great idea.

The rest is history. No longer would people look at the roof of an RV as an afterthought. From now on, they'd see it as a whole new living space. Owing to Frank's awareness, he was able to make a major breakthrough and launch his dream business. Frank's story reminds us a bit of one of our favorite fables: the story of Jerry Schwartz. Ever heard of Jerry Schwartz? We hadn't either until a friend told us this story.

THE STORY OF JERRY SCHWARTZ

Thousands of years ago, a group of escaped slaves were making their way across a parched desert in search of their homeland. Every day, the slaves sent scouts ahead in search of water. One day, a scout came around a bend in the trail and saw a tree on fire.

"Wow," the scout thought to himself. "It's so hot out here, trees are just bursting into flames." He continued on the trail without thinking another thought about what he had just seen.

An hour later, another scout hiked up the same trail and rounded the same bend. The bush—burning hot and bright—was just a few feet away from him. Instead of walking on as the scout before him had, this one stood transfixed by the burning bush. "Wow. This must be a sign from God. What can it mean?" he thought.

Who was the scout who saw a greater meaning in the burning bush? Moses, of course. The other scout? Well, that was Jerry Schwartz. We all know who Moses is. But Jerry has faded into obscurity. The lesson behind this little story? If you're open-minded and aware of your surroundings, you too may find inspiration—and opportunity—in the most unexpected places.

Protecting Your Idea

Patent protection is essential for anyone who wants to commercialize a new idea or to start up a company based on a novel technology or product. Small businesses account for a disproportionate amount of the "economically and technically important" inventions that are created each year, according to a survey by the Small Business Administration. The survey, conducted in 2003, showed that although small businesses generate only 6 percent of patents, they make up 14 percent of the most important ones.

That's great news for entrepreneurs. But patenting an idea, innovation, or process can be expensive, tricky, and time-consuming. In this section, we highlight some things first-time patent filers should know about. We asked for advice from Nick Godici, the commissioner for patents at the U.S. Patent and Trademark Office, and William Abbatt, a patent attorney with Brooks & Kushman in Southfield, Michigan. Before you decide to file a patent application, we suggest you visit the website for the U.S. Patent and Trademark Office, www.uspto.gov. Also, we recommend consulting your own patent attorney, who'll be uniquely qualified to draft and prosecute your patent application.

First, what should you patent? Patents cover new, useful, and nonobvious inventions or processes. Patents generally protect things you can use, or at least touch and feel, like Frank Messano's SkyDeck. But they can also cover a process, such as Amazon.com's "one-click shopping," or improvements on products that have already been patented. Once awarded, a patent allows you to prevent others from making, using, or selling your invention. Patents don't cover intellectual property such as brand names or written works. Two other instruments within intellectual property law cover those areas. A trademark keeps others from using your brand. A trademark covers a name, symbol, or logo and is used to distinguish between goods and services. Copyrights cover artistic and written works, such as this book, and prevent people from copying your works.

How do you patent your invention? You or your attorney start by conducting a patent search to determine the likelihood that you'll be able to obtain patent coverage. If you want to do some research on your own, you can search electronically for pertinent patents via the Internet. "Every single patent is available for search online," Nick Godici says.

Once your preliminary search is completed and you decide to move forward with the patent application, your attorney will prepare the forms, which will include sections of drawings, descriptions, and, most important, a list of what are known as the "claims." The real power of a patent is in this claims section of the application, says attorney Bill Abbatt, and should be the section to which you pay the most attention. There's a balancing act in writing claims, according to Bill. "You want the broadest possible coverage for your patent. But you don't want it to be so broad that it won't qualify with a patent examiner."

Once the patent application is filed, a patent examiner is assigned to your patent. He or she can send the patent back to you many times over the course of about two years—the average time it takes for a patent to be issued—asking for more information and advising you of problems they see with the patent. Patents are turned down for several reasons. The first is "prior art," which means that it's been previously created or explored by some other person. But keep in mind that "prior art" doesn't refer only to other patents covering your idea. Prior art can come in the form of people discussing the idea in magazines or trade journals. A second reason is that the idea is obvious—you can't patent the wheel. Third, it has to have some "utility," meaning that the patent should be useful.

What's a provisional patent versus a regular patent? In fact, there's no such thing as a "provisional patent." There *is* a provisional patent *application* that can serve as a placeholder for your invention. It requires less information than a formal patent application. The provisional application is less expensive to file and is never seen by a patent examiner. And the claims section is not as critical a component as that in a formal application.

Provisional applications are useful in certain instances. Say you have an invention you want to patent but you need to show it off at a trade show that is just a week away. Using a provisional application "will help preserve your idea and get the ball rolling," says patent commissioner Godici. But provisional applications come with big risks. "Remember that all the subject matter in that provisional application is final. Let's say you decide to convert the provisional to a formal application later that year. All the claims you make in the formal application must be supported in that first provisional application," Godici says. You should note that a provisional application lasts for only one year. You must file a formal patent application covering the idea disclosed in your provisional application within that year or you lose your right to obtain patent coverage on what you disclosed in the provisional application.

In addition, if your provisional application skimps on the claims, you may find that someone else has come along and filed a patent application that covers everything *but* those claims, thereby limiting your commercial opportunity. Bill Abbatt's advice on provisionals? Use them sparingly and convert them as quickly as possible to a formal patent application so your invention is truly covered.

How long do patents last? Twenty years from the date of filing of the application, but there are specific dates and fee schedules that you must keep track of to keep your patent active during those 20 years. Note: During the patent application process, which can take two years or more, you can put "patent pending" on your literature as a way to notify people that you have first dibs on the idea. Once your patent is issued, you must remove the "patent pending" notice and replace it with the issued patent number. To see our first issued patent, #4,902,956, visit startup-nation.com/patents, where we also provide additional helpful information about patents.

CHAPTER FIVE

Creating the Perfect Business Plan for Yourself

Mad Scientist Crafts Business Plan

We vividly remember our first meeting with a brilliant but slightly "mad" scientist, Bill MacArthur. It was 1997, and a researcher at one of our biotech companies had suggested we grab lunch with Bill, his former University of Michigan roommate, to listen to his ideas about starting up a new biotech company called Geneworks. As it was described to us, Geneworks' technology involved a revolutionary method for producing the key ingredients in human pharmaceuticals. Bill apparently had developed a concept to genetically reprogram chickens so they'd lay eggs containing the key ingredients. We thought we'd heard just about everything in our years helping inventors and scientists, but that one took the cake. Let's just say that Bill's concept sounded a little bit farfetched.

Frankly, Bill just reinforced that concern when he showed up at the restaurant for our lunch meeting. He arrived in a tattered T-shirt and shorts. His hair conjured up images of Einstein, frizzy and wild, and he had this intense gleam in his eye. We exchanged a secret Sloan-brother-to-brother glance: What have we gotten ourselves into?!

But then Bill started talking.

Rich

I immediately realized we were sitting in the company of a genius. He was so passionate, so versed in his science. But what really blew us away was the background Bill shared with us about how he had kept his research and the prospects for the technology moving forward. Apparently, after having spent years developing his technology, Bill was blindsided by news that he would not be allowed to commercialize his technology without a license to practice veterinary medicine.

Refusing to let anything stand in his way, without thinking twice, Bill immediately enrolled in vet school, graduated four years later, and became Dr. Bill MacArthur, DVM. It was just a short time later that we found ourselves enrapt by his story over lunch. I was struck by the degree of his commitment to make Geneworks happen. He had the tenacity we always look for in entrepreneurs.

We'll admit, Bill basically fried our brains that day. We were lost in talk of genes, proteins, antibodies, molecular structures, viral vectors, retroviruses, and what was going on in the beakers inside his university lab. It took us a good two hours of conversation before we began to understand the gist of Bill's idea and how it could be packaged into a business that was viable. By the time we left Bill that day, we were hooked on the science, hooked on the business potential, and hooked on Bill's passion and drive.

There was just one problem.

Bill had no idea how to transform his idea into a viable business plan, let alone how to run a business. He was the quintessential scientist. He didn't have a team or any idea of how he was going to fund the launch and operation of the business. He was working out of a borrowed lab and quickly running out of the

$50,000 in cash he'd raised from friends and family. While Bill had spent huge amounts of time working on his science, he'd spent no time at all thinking about how he was going to run the business that would turn his idea into a commercial success.

A few days after that first meeting, we sat down in our offices with Bill to begin sketching out a plan to create a business out of his idea. First, we needed to figure out what kind of business Geneworks should be. Should it be a full-blown pharmaceutical company that would produce medicines using the new technology and then sell those medicines to the public? Should it develop the technology and then license it to companies who would in turn pay Geneworks a royalty? Or should it produce the key ingredients using Bill's proprietary technology and then sell those ingredients to the pharmaceutical companies? The more we brainstormed with Bill and guided him through the process of thinking through the possible business models, the clearer it became: Geneworks would be a manufacturing company.

It would produce the ingredients through its unique system of manufacturing and ship them to its customers, the pharmaceutical companies, in much the same way an automotive supplier would produce and supply parts to the automotive companies. The technology was complicated, but now at least we had arrived at a simple business model to bring it to market. Once we understood and agreed upon the basic business model, we were ready to create the business plan that would make the model work.

Bill recalls, "What once seemed so complicated, now seemed tangible. The Sloans helped me see my idea in the context of a simple business model, and then we worked together to craft a business plan to take out all of the mystery for me." In the end, $18 million was raised to fund Geneworks, enough money for Bill to prove the science, create flocks of customized chickens, house them in ultramodern facilities, and conduct business with big-league pharma companies. "Without the business plan, we could never have raised that kind of money," said Bill, "let alone have ever gotten off the ground."

No matter how extraordinary your idea is—and Bill's idea certainly was—it's not going to make for a successful business until you've worked out virtually every detail of how you're going to run the operation. What's the basic business model? How much funding will you need? How are you going to make money? How big is the market? Who's the competition and how are you going to beat them? What kind of a team will you need? These and a host of other questions must be answered first before you can really say you're "open for business."

That's why we're huge proponents of the process of preparing a business plan.

The Defining Dozen: Twelve Questions That Lay the Groundwork for a Business Plan That Works

Whether you're like Bill MacArthur and seeking millions, or you're interested in opening up a home-based freelance public relations business, or perhaps rebuilding and selling engines from an auto garage, *you need a solid business plan.*

Why? Because no matter how modest or complex your business is, your plan will set a course for you to reach your hopes and dreams. You already established a Life Plan in Chapter Three. Now you're going to create a business plan that moves you closer to living the life you desire.

A business plan makes real the fantasy of running your own business. This is where you start to ask tough questions, to analyze your idea from all angles, to really construct the business case for your idea or your innovation or your service and how you'll make money from the effort that lies ahead. The very process of creating a business plan is a huge confidence-builder. It replaces questions and confusion with answers and a sense that you can do this! You'll truly understand the market in which your business will operate. You'll also develop a strategy to carve out your own opportunity in that market. You'll craft a business model to capture that market in a way that supports the lifestyle you want to lead. Equipped with this confidence and know-how, you'll embark on a journey with a road map that'll keep you on course.

To get you started, we've put together twelve questions—we call them "the defining dozen"—that'll help you establish a foundation for your business plan. This is another great time for you to pull out that notebook or boot up the computer and log your answers. You probably won't use all of what you write down in your formal business plan, but don't throw anything away. You may want to review these thoughts when you update your business plan down the road. We often find that these early brainstorms are ripe with ideas about future products and services.

Now to the questions:

1. **What's your idea?** In simple, straightforward terms, write down what your business idea is. If you can't explain the essence of your idea quickly and simply, keep working on it until you can. Complicated, jargon-filled descriptions are real turnoffs. Someone listening should be able to say immediately, "Oh. I get it." If we had tried to say, "Geneworks is an avian transgenics company that will revolutionize the pharmaceutical industry by modifying chickens' DNA using viral vectors designed to genetically replace ovalbumin (pronounced

QUICK TIP

Bake Your Idea in the Oven

Creating a business plan is so important that we dedicated an entire room in our office to just this purpose. We call it the "Oven" for the heat that always seems to build up in there during brainstorming sessions. The walls are floor-to-ceiling white boards, and everything you write on them can be recorded and saved digitally—in whatever colors you use. The solid door has a lock accessible only from the inside. Pizzas are often delivered directly to the Oven—the door opens, pizzas are handed in, money is exchanged, the door shuts. Click. The door is relocked. People who've spent a day or two in the Oven say it's brainstorming heaven. Free from distraction. A blank canvas for creativity. Totally wired. And everything is captured for future use.

To make sure your business planning is as productive as possible, find a space where you can go to concentrate, collaborate, tap into the Internet, and preserve your brainstorms for future use.

'ohv-al-byumin') in the egg whites of their eggs with proprietary proteins and antibodies," we would never have gotten the attention of investors. But tell them, "It's basically a manufacturing business that produces key ingredients for pharmaceutical companies at a lower-than-average cost" and now you're talking business talk. Your description must highlight the qualities that distinguish your idea. In the case of Geneworks, it was the ability to produce the ingredients at a lower cost.

2. **How does your idea address a need?** This is where you get to explore the true potential of your new idea. There are two basic types of demand in the marketplace—a "want" and a "need." A business that addresses a need is always more promising than one that addresses a want. In the case of a market need, there's pre-existing "pent-up" demand, and creating awareness is all that's required to catalyze the sales of your offering. A market need creates "pull" in the marketplace, and the end user literally pulls your product or service through the system to satisfy his or her need. In the case of a market want, you'll be required to "push" your product onto consumers, and this usually requires expensive advertising and marketing campaigns in order to encourage and influence the sale. There are varying degrees of "want" in the marketplace so try to get a sense of the degree to which the market wants your product or service. Obviously the more the "want" approaches "need," the better. Basic food and shelter are examples of market needs while goods like jewelry, video games, and even gourmet food products are examples of market wants.

What want or need does your product or service address, and how? Why is it the best solution for addressing that need? Figure out if your idea is revolutionary,

evolutionary, or simply a copycat. A revolutionary idea, something that really is different, often means you have far greater chance for upside—more potential revenue and profits. But revolutions typically come with a lot of risk. Don't underestimate how challenging it is to educate consumers and change their behavior before they see the need for your product. It's often said among seasoned entrepreneurs that you can easily spot pioneers. They're the ones with all the arrows in their backs. Be clear in your business plan about how much pioneering you'll have to do before people understand how and why your product is a winner.

An evolutionary idea typically has less upside than a revolutionary one, but your odds are better of getting the business up and running and into a stable mode relatively fast. With an evolutionary idea, the bigger burden is making clear to your customers that which distinguishes you from the rest of the competition.

3. **What model suits you best?** As we saw with Bill MacArthur and his company Geneworks, figuring out the right business model is critical to your success. Take another look at the discussion of business models in Chapter Four to think this through. Or do a little "recon" in your hometown or perhaps on the Internet. Investigate business models that other people have used when selling a similar kind of product or service. It's great to be innovative, but tread lightly when being innovative with unproven business models. You might find yourself rewinding to the "dot-bomb" era.

Figure out a business format that best fits your Life Plan and offers the most direct route to success with the biggest potential payoff. The clearer your business model is, the easier it will be to figure out your revenue model. As we saw with Bill's business, the model you choose can dramatically change when, how, and in what form you generate revenue.

4. **What's so different about what you offer?** To answer this question, repeat after us: research, research, and research! You can almost bet that someone's going to come up to you as you're charting a course to get into business and say, "Hey, did you know that XYZ Company does exactly what you do?"

If you're prepared, you'll be able to answer, "Yes, I do know them, but this is how we're different." You have to be master of your domain—*the expert.*

That's especially important when it comes to warming up investors and selling to customers. Remember that investors will want to know why they should invest in your company rather than the guy down the street. But don't overhype your differences. Pick the ones that you can really *prove* and substantiate. It may be that one simple but profound distinction will be enough to create a *cha-ching!* So don't waste time drumming up weak distinctions—rely on the strongest and lose the rest. Also, remember that the differences don't have to be rooted in a complicated technological advantage or some mysterious "secret sauce." Often, a difference stems from simply executing better than anyone else. Take Peter Romero, president of Del Mar Environmental Services and a "Super Startup" guest on a 2004 radio show we broadcasted from center stage at the Fortune Small Business Conference in Chicago. Peter's business is asbestos removal.

We asked him what was different about Del Mar compared to his competitors and how he had managed to be so successful in such a competitive business. Without hesitation, he answered with a siren song about customer service. "I love my business when I see my customers smile," he said. And that's Peter's difference. He actually cares about the people in the houses and buildings he's clearing of asbestos, and he lets them know that. That simple but powerful treatment of his customers gives him his advantage over his competition and has led to tens of millions in lucrative contracts over the years and many business awards in his community.

5. **How big is the market and how big will you grow?** Exploring the market and understanding the growth potential for your idea is essential. To get a handle on this, you have to understand the demographics of people in your target market. Distill those people into categories of low level of need, medium level of need, and high level of need for your offering. You can actually construct a target, like the archery target you may have tried to hit as a kid (the one with the concentric circles). Except the "bull's-eye" in this case is your sweet spot—the *target* market that will be the focus of your initial marketing and sales efforts. Once you've penetrated that inner circle, you can grow bigger by broadening your offerings and your marketing and sales efforts to include the people with a medium level of need and so on.

To get a fix on the degree of need that may exist for what you're going to offer, try to figure out which market is easiest to penetrate. Is the market growing? If so, by how much? Can you figure out if the market is already saturated, mature, or shrinking? We find that a great deal of the information you'll need can be readily gathered over the Internet. The information you'll find there comes free in some cases, but there are also studies online that have been performed by major consulting firms. These studies are often purchasable and can be really helpful in facilitating a deeper understanding of a market and your opportunity within it. When a company really understands its markets, it can tackle them methodically.

Researching your growth potential will give you a sense of how big your company can be as well as help you set targets for rolling out new products.

A note of caution: Don't get caught using "Chinese math." It's all too easy to pile up grandiose numbers for your market size. The phrase "Chinese math" was used back in the 1990s during an era when consumer product companies were eyeing the billions of consumers in China. But eyeing was about all they could really do. Even though there were billions of potential consumers there, they remained just that—*potential*, not real. This was largely because there was no viable way to get access to them.

Let's say you wanted to market water purifiers to remote Chinese peasants. Their need was certainly extreme. But they lived down dusty roads in villages, crowded into bare-bones homes without TVs, magazines, or billboards. And since they commuted to work on bicycles, radio advertising was also out of the question. Not to mention that China was still mired in a strict form of communism; freedom of information and disposable income were hard to come by. Even though the market was vast, the obstacles for selling water purifiers to those *potential* customers would have been insurmountable.

Avoid using "Chinese math" in your market estimates. Get real about how many people there are in your market—and about whether you can reach them effectively.

6. **What's your role going to be?** To answer this question, go back to your Life Plan. Review all the activities you love to do and the kinds of skills that you enjoy using. Maybe you'll realize for the first time that you don't want to go into this business alone. Maybe you'll want your role to center on the "people kind of stuff" and leave the mechanics and "back of house" tasks to a partner or a key employee. You might decide to be the chief technology officer, because what you're really good at is innovating. Your Life Plan should provide a great starting point for you to understand if your bailiwick is managing people, product development, or selling like there's no tomorrow.

Whether you're going the solo route or you've determined

you'll build a team, this next piece of advice is critically important: Make a list of duties and responsibilities. Remember, it's very easy in a business to become overwhelmed by all the work piling up in your inbox. Leave yourself enough breathing space to enjoy being in business for yourself. By writing down your own job description, you can free yourself from duties that aren't the best use of your time. Be true to yourself; your business will suffer if you take on roles that you either don't enjoy or that don't fit your interests and your skills.

7. **Who's on your team?** This is where thinking about your team members comes in. One of the key factors that'll separate your business from the competition will be the people you choose to work with. Give serious review to the team you pick to start and run your business. Your success depends in large part on them.

Your business plan is the place to sort out your areas of expertise. Maybe you do have a great idea in a market you don't know much about. If this is the case, hire someone who has expertise in that market. Or like Bill at Geneworks, who spent four years learning to be a vet, spend the time getting the expertise and credentials you need. In a formal business plan, investors will want to know that you and your team have a deep knowledge of the business.

If you won't be hiring a lot of people right at first, we still suggest you write up a wish list of folks that you'd like to hire. We'll talk more about this in Chapter Seven, but it really helps to have a dream team waiting in the wings. Finally, if you're going it alone, don't forget to write down how you plan to outsource work that you simply can't do yourself.

8. **How will customers buy from you, and how much will they pay?** Outline in detail just how you plan to get your product or service out to the market. This includes describing how you're going to manufacture your product and how you'll

deliver it. Will it be sold over the Internet or from the shelves of your own Main Street store? Will you have distribution into the "big box" retailers or use a national network of sales reps? Just remember that you must have a well-defined and achievable plan in order to get what you're selling in front of your customers.

And what about price? It's a critical component of success. Price your offering too high and nobody will buy your product. Price it too low and you might be leaving money on the table, or, worse yet, you might not make any money at all. Cheryl Tallman, whom we feature as Super Startup #3 later in the book, started a company called Fresh Baby. What Cheryl did to position her products for success perfectly demonstrates the importance of appropriate pricing. She wanted to make sure that the prices for her freezable trays for fresh baby food and mother's milk were below those of her well-known competitor Tupperware; she knew a lower price would differentiate her product. But the manufacturing cost of an initial run of 2,000 trays was relatively high. So instead of pricing her trays based on the cost of the initial manufacturing quantity, she asked her supplier how much a run of 50,000 would be.

In the higher volume, the unit price came way down.

"I took into account those extremes in price and picked a price in the middle. It was a price where I could still make money but undercut Tupperware's pricing." This meant Cheryl would lose money on those first 2,000, but as soon as the volume of sales increased she'd be making good profit margins overall. Cheryl's story conveys perfectly why you should consider your customers closely. Figure out what price your customer would pay for the product and determine if you can offer better customer service than your competitors. Never, ever forget who pays the bills—*your customers.*

9. **How much money do you need and how much will you**

make? Now's the time to start mulling over your financials. The two fundamental ingredients here are the expenditures required to transform your idea into a viable, operating business and the revenues that that business will generate. You'll start by thumbnailing how much you'll spend on things like facilities (be it a retail store or a home office), product development, travel, legal fees, inventory, office supplies, marketing, and salaries for your employees. Be thorough. Talk to other people in your field, join an entrepreneur networking group in your industry, and pick their brains about how much it cost them to get started.

Then rough out your revenue projections. This should be the exhilarating part. It's when you start to see how your idea will turn into actual dollars. Although this will be exciting, don't project outlandish revenues. You're setting yourself up for failure if you do. First, you'll feel less than successful if you don't meet those revenue targets at the end of the year. Second, overhyped revenue projections may lead to hiring too many people or building up huge inventories that you can't sell. Third, if you base your company's valuation on those revenues and don't meet those goals, you'll severely damage your credibility with the money people and your future money-raising prospects. Take our advice—*underpromise* and *overdeliver*. You'll feel like a star if you exceed your revenue projections and you'll have more money in the bank to reinvest in your company's future.

Lastly, don't forget to identify when you expect revenues to be received versus when you expect expenses to hit. This is a basic form of a cash flow analysis designed to let you know if and when you'll need to access additional capital in order to keep the business alive. If the capital required exceeds what you have available, that means you'll have to raise some money.

QUICK TIP

Meet and Greet!

Get out and get "into the mix." Talk to entrepreneurs who've funded their company successfully and ask how they did it and who their sources of money were. Maybe they'll introduce you to their banker or their angel investor—who knows!

Also, join your local entrepreneur networking groups. Mingling there can lead you to introductions that can really catalyze your financing efforts. The money people can also be found through referrals by high-powered attorneys and accountants. It might also help to meet with a financial advisor at your local Small Business Development Center, which is affiliated with the Small Business Administration. Lastly, you can visit startupnation.com to participate in message boards with fellow entrepreneurs.

10. **Where's the startup money coming from?** By answering No. 9, you'll learn two of the most important things you'll need to know when answering Question No. 10. You'll learn how much money you need and how much you think you're going to make. Now start thinking about where to get the capital to get your business off the ground. We'll go into detail on this in Chapter Six, but in this prep stage, consider sources such as banks, friends, family, and angels.

If you plan on getting your money through venture capitalists, determine a valuation for your company. More often than not, as in the residential real estate market, the valuation of your company will be heavily influenced by the value of comparables—valuations of companies at a similar stage of development with similar characteristics. Knowing the valuation helps you figure out how much of the company's equity you'll have to provide in return for the capital influx.

11. **How will you measure success?** For so many people, money made is the big measurement of success. But while financial achievements will be fundamental to your business's viability, there's more to gain from running a business than just making money. It's important to define what success means to you, as we discussed in Chapter Three. We measure success through the StartupNation Manifesto, which keeps us grounded in our ideas of work as freedom, work as family, and work as fulfillment. What will yours be? As part of the business-planning process, consider how you'll define success.

12. **What are your key milestones?** Create a chart that shows dates when you expect to achieve key milestones as your business launches and grows.

Have a visual map of what has to happen—*and when*—to keep you focused on priorities. While many times your guesstimates of a major milestone will be off the mark, those milestones are important because they'll keep you accountable as you evaluate your progress. If you're not hitting your key milestones, it'll force you to get real about your performance, your resources, and the resolve you'll need to get back on track. You may decide that a "plan B" shift in thinking is required. But without the milestone chart, you'll never know if you need to shift or respond until it's way too late.

Once you've dealt with these Defining Dozen questions, you'll be much further along in teeing up a great business plan. Hopefully, you have lots of notes that can be cut and pasted directly into your formal business plan. Most of all, we hope that you're feeling more informed and confident now that you're well versed about your opportunity.

Now let's get under way with the crafting of the formal plan.

The Formal Business Plan

You're now ready to bring it all together. You can begin preparing your all-important formal business plan. Designed and used correctly, this plan will become the strategic backbone of your dream business. The structure we provide should help you manage your business on a day-to-day basis, prioritize your time and resources, provide a guidepost for monitoring your progress, and help you make adjustments as you go along. The process of preparing your business plan will also get you more organized and focused than ever, helping you to tackle the challenges ahead. In fact, it'll force you to identify and address the obstacles you'll confront before you ever start up. And if you need to raise funds, you'll have an invaluable tool to use when meeting with the money people.

QUICK TIP

Write Your Executive Summary Last

StartupNation's COO John Siverling offers the following advice: The executive summary is the part of your business plan investors read first, but it should be the last section you write. Too many entrepreneurs start with the summary as a shortcut, and never properly develop the building blocks. Focus first on fully developing each section of the business plan, including all of the support materials. Once those sections are complete, the executive summary almost writes itself.

A few notes: First, length. We often get asked, "How long should my business plan be?" There are no hard-and-fast rules. It's the substance that makes the difference between a mediocre plan and one that's destined for success.

Second, avoid getting too rigid. As your business grows, your business plan should change and probably expand. We've seen plans that were nothing more than three handwritten pages and others that stretched over a hundred typed pages with all sorts of exhibits tagged on.

Third, if you're going to be sharing your plan with financiers or any outside parties, *looks matter*. We hate to say it, but from the cover letter to the tabs between sections, you have to make sure your plan looks like it means business! As they say, a first impression goes a long way, and that impression you make on your dream investor could be the difference between a funded business primed to take off and a flat-out "no thanks." Take into account whether the information is presented in a way that's clear and easy to navigate, and that shows some of the personality of your business. Using charts, photos, and graphics can all be very helpful. Be proud of this document. It holds all of your hopes and dreams for a successful business.

Executive Summary

This is the section of the plan that'll be read first by investors. It's basically the first two to four pages of the plan, and it highlights the key points and data inside the body of the business plan. If investors become curious after reading the executive summary, they'll dive into the inner detailed pages and scan for answers to specific questions they might have. It'll take discipline to keep the executive summary this short, but it's a must. Give special attention to the need in the marketplace and how your business best fulfills that need. Put emphasis on the great people who are involved. *This includes you*—this is your chance to establish your credibility. Write in clear, concise language. Stay away from jargon. Conclude the executive summary by providing a statement about the amount of financing you need and the basic deal terms you're offering. (If your financier will be a bank, you won't need to include deal terms.) They'll never turn the page if they don't believe in the case you make for your business. Lastly, it's a good idea to write your executive summary after you've completed the body of the plan. This will allow you to pull out the most compelling points and facts from the text and use them to create a slam-dunk opener.

Business Description

This area is reserved for a complete and detailed description of your business. Include what you offer and why it is distinct and desirable. Contrast what you plan to offer from what the competition offers. Provide that information in the context of the business model you've chosen. Explain that model and how it works. List important strategic assets such as key relationships, a distribution opportunity, a website you've already created, and patents or any important intellectual property. Describe your facilities, whether this is a home-based business or a dedicated space you rent or own. Discuss your key suppliers. List your strategic partners, including marketing and manufacturing partners. After someone reads this section of the plan, they should be able to "get" what you're offering with total clarity.

Market Analysis

This section is where your research into the market and industry can really pay off. Site your source. Provide a simple description of the market, the need, and the potential growth opportunities you see for your business. Then show off all the research you've done. Pour it on! Give facts and figures. Cite your sources. Point out unusual trends you've noticed or untapped niches you believe your offering will serve. Give a conservative and credible prediction on the growth of the market. This is another place to be wary of making outlandish predictions.

Definitely talk about your competitors. We often hear from entrepreneurs that they don't like discussing the competition, particularly in a business plan. They think if there are competitors already doing what they do, then no one will be interested in their product or service. But acknowledging the competition shows that you've thoroughly investigated the market and that you have confidence in your superiority. In a subsection of your market analysis, you can put in a chart comparing the competition's offerings versus yours. That will show how you're going to be able to trounce your competition and will underscore the appeal of your business opportunity.

Marketing and Distribution

At this point, you start making your case. You have to impress your reader with the marketing and distribution strategies.

To do so, start by telling how your service or product addresses the market opportunity. Show off your marketing moxie with ideas that'll create awareness and persuade consumers to buy your product or service. This is where your passion about your business idea should shine through. Really hammer home your competitive advantages. Include plans for marketing, advertising, and public relations in detail, emphasizing any ideas you believe are new and novel about the strategy.

Give a schedule of when you're going to achieve certain levels of awareness, demand, and distribution. If it'll be a year or more before your offering is fully in the market making a difference, be clear about that—you and your investors need to know if it'll take time for your product to be available. Be clear on how you'll deliver your product.

Personnel

Don't forget your people! If you envision a business built around you as a solo act, that's fine. But are there key relationships you'll need to have? Maybe you plan to outsource certain functions or partner up in key areas of your business. Maybe you have the support of a great group of advisors who are willing to lend their names and their counsel to the business.

If you anticipate hiring people into the organization, list their roles and qualifications, including their education, experience, and accomplishments. Even if you don't plan to bring these people in initially, it's good to provide as complete a list as possible of the employees you know you'll eventually have and what their roles and responsibilities will be.

Exit Strategy

The exit strategy, driven by your Life Plan, describes the ultimate destiny of the business. Understanding what happens at the point you're ready to exit the business could impact the way you operate the business in the early stages. Or you may want to pass the reins of your business to your children someday. It could lead you to try to grow at a blistering pace and sell within a few years to another company.

Venture capitalists and angels love the financial windfall that can come from this kind of exit. Or perhaps you're more intent on building a moderately paced "lifestyle" business that has a slow fuse and much less pressure associated with it.

Don't Buy into Your Own Hype!

Can you picture the guy who claims he's going to sell a million units of his widget but he doesn't even have distribution in place? Or how about one of those dot-com companies that threw away $2 million on a 60-second Super Bowl commercial, believing it would somehow catapult them to success? We all know otherwise. . . .

It's tough to balance your enthusiasm and passion with reality. But make no mistake: It's dangerous to buy into your own hype when running a business. It can lead you to buying too much inventory, renting too much space, hiring too many people, and spending too much on nonessentials.

Instead, weigh in with advisors about your bold ideas. Have a checks-and-balances process to keep you smart and on course.

The good news is that whatever your exit strategy is, it's something you can choose before you ever get into business. And that allows you to establish a course, set expectations, and have the security that comes from knowing what the end goal is for the business you're starting up.

The Financials

A financial analysis is important whether or not you ever plan on asking for money from an investor. If we stick with our analogy that a business plan serves as the backbone of your company, money is the blood that keeps your business alive. We'll get even more in-depth about money—creating just the right mix of capital in a method we call the Goldilocks Approach—Chapter Six. But here we'll cover the financial information you should include in your business plan. The Financial section should map out the first few years of business and contain these items:

- Written narrative of key business assumptions
- Income Statement
- Balance Sheet
- Statement of cash flows
- Cash Management Report

Some of these terms may be unfamiliar to you. Depending on how you want to use your business plan, we might recommend that you add to this list. For example, we'd recommend you include a discussion of valuation if you'll be using this business plan as a tool to raise money.

In your written narrative of key assumptions, outline what will drive your business's performance over your first few years, including things like key hires and their salaries. Include an explanation of any significant capital expenses. Also, describe the equations you used to figure out your projected revenues. Yes, there's a lot of detailed, technical stuff to do here. But it's going to force you to think through the logic behind your numbers and position you to truly understand your business. Fully equipped with this knowledge, you'll be able to think and communicate strategically.

The narrative can be mostly bullet points with quick-hitting, no-nonsense language. (Save the glorious verbiage for your sales pitches!)

For example, you might indicate,

- Marketing = approximately 10% of total expenditures in Year 1

After seeing that assumption, the reader would understand how you arrived at your budget allocation for marketing for the first year of your business.

If what we're asking you to provide here is out of your comfort zone, you might want to find a good accountant who can help you work up the key assumptions as well as the rest of the financials. When we first started out, neither of us knew much about financial analysis. Like most entrepreneurs, we didn't have MBAs. But over time we learned.

When contracting with someone to help you with your numbers and assumptions, just be sure you don't entirely remove yourself from the process. You've got to have a grasp on the concept and contents that drive the financial reality of your business in order to be an effective entrepreneur.

It's important to include projections in your business plan so you and others can get an idea about how you expect your business to perform. But projections are just *projections*—entrepreneurs often think money will come in sooner and in greater amounts than what actually occurs. To avoid running into trouble later, we recommend that you prepare a best-, mid-, and worst-case set of projections so that you can see a range of possible revenue outcomes. Look at your worst-case scenario and make sure you've made provisions so your business will be able to survive even in the most pessimistic case.

You can review more in-depth information about financial projection spreadsheets at www.startupnation.com/financials, but we provide some basic details here to get you in the zone about definitions and uses.

Income statement: Shows a summary of revenues, cost of goods sold, and expenses. Also referred to as your "profit-and-loss" or "P&L" statement.

Balance sheet: Shows a snapshot of your financial status at a point in time. It includes your liabilities, assets, and shareholder equity.

Statement of cash flows: Shows historical cash-flow performance of your business. This traditional accounting report is the best financial tool to analyze how cash was earned and how cash was used by operating, financing, and investing activities.

In contrast to the statement of cash flows—which looks back in time—we've developed a critically important instrument to help you forecast and manage your cash today and into the future. It's something we've coined a **cash management report.** It was originally introduced to us by Chris Cameron, an ongoing partner of ours in our venture development activities and a successful entrepreneur in his own right. The cash management report is a simple but powerful time-tested tool that's extremely effective in helping you manage your cash. It looks at how cash moves in and out of a business on a monthly basis. As you can see in the example on the next page, by preparing a cash management report before the launch of your business, you'll be able to determine *if* you'll need to raise outside capital, *when* you'll need it, and *how much* will be required.

Here are some assumptions that the founder of "Newco," a company that sells "widgets" to other companies, used in building his cash management report:

Working Capital

- Starting Cash = $100,000
- $25,000 Line of Credit with Bank, secured by Inventory, Accounts Receivable, and second mortgage on home

Inventory

- We will build up inventory to start selling in the first month of operations, two months ahead of revenues.

So, what can we learn from the cash management report for Newco? We can learn that if Newco starts up with $100,000 and has a $25,000 line of credit with the bank, the business can support its operations given the planned cash expenditures, the projected cash receipts, the planned borrowings, and the starting capital. And we can see that the business breaks even beginning in November. That's the point that Newco becomes "cash flow positive." This gives the company the freedom to either repay borrowings or invest in the growth of the business. In June we see a need to dip into the bank line of credit. This is largely due to the large expenditure up front to build up inventory and pay for necessary capital expenditures. By the end of the year, however,

NEWCO
CASH MANAGEMENT REPORT—2005 BUDGETED

	Jan	Feb	Mar	Apr	May	Jun	Jul	Aug	Sep	Oct	Nov	Dec	2005 Total
Cash Expenditures													
Inventory Purchases	40,000	–	11,700	14,370	19,560	16,500	20,940	6,450	23,610	19,740	26,340	54,600	253,810
Wages & Benefits	8,500	8,500	8,500	8,500	8,500	8,500	8,500	8,500	8,500	8,500	8,500	8,500	102,000
Marketing	4,500	3,500	3,500	4,500	4,500	4,500	2,500	2,500	4,500	4,500	1,500	1,500	42,000
Travel	1,500	1,500	1,500	1,500	1,500	1,500	1,500	1,500	1,500	1,500	1,500	1,500	18,000
Administrative	1,250	1,250	1,250	1,250	1,250	1,250	1,250	1,250	1,250	1,250	1,250	1,250	15,000
Rent & Office Supplies	3,000	1,500	1,500	1,500	1,500	1,500	1,500	1,500	1,500	1,500	1,500	1,500	19,500
Capital Purchases	3,000	–	–	–	–	–	–	–	–	–	–	–	3,000
Miscellaneous	150	150	150	150	150	150	150	150	150	150	150	150	1,800
Total Cash Expenditures	61,900	16,400	28,100	31,770	36,960	33,900	36,340	21,850	41,010	37,140	40,740	69,000	455,110
Notes Payable Repaid													
Line of Credit	–	–	–	–	–	–	–	–	–	–	–	20,000	20,000
Total Cash Expenditures	61,900	16,400	28,100	31,770	36,960	33,900	36,340	21,850	41,010	37,140	40,740	69,000	475,110
Cash Receipts													
Customer A	–	–	15,500	–	15,500	–	15,500	–	25,000	–	30,000	50,000	151,500
Customer B	–	–	2,500	1,750	3,500	1,500	5,000	250	750	3,300	1,400	2,500	22,450
Customer C	–	–	–	–	–	5,000	–	–	–	–	–	–	5,000
Customer D	–	–	–	14,200	13,600	13,000	14,400	2,500	13,600	13,600	12,500	14,500	111,900
Customer E	–	–	1,500	8,000	–	8,000	–	8,000	–	16,000	–	24,000	65,500
Investors	–	–	–	–	–	–	–	–	–	–	–	–	–
Interest	–	–	–	–	–	–	–	–	–	–	–	–	–
Total Cash Receipts	–	–	19,500	23,950	32,600	27,500	34,900	10,750	39,350	32,900	43,900	91,000	356,350
Notes Payable Borrowings													
Line of Credit	–	–	–	–	–	10,000	–	10,000	–	5,000	–	–	25,000
Net Change in Cash	(61,900)	(16,400)	(8,600)	(7,820)	(4,360)	3,600	(1,440)	(1,100)	(1,660)	760	3,160	2,000	
Cash Beginning of Month	100,000	38,100	21,700	13,100	5,280	920	4,520	3,080	1,980	320	1,080	4,240	
Projected Cash End of Month	38,100	21,700	13,100	5,280	920	4,520	3,080	1,980	320	1,080	4,240	6,240	
Beginning Cash	100,000												

nearly all of the line of credit is paid off and the business is financing itself. So if all goes exactly as planned, the founder of Newco is sitting pretty.

But you can also see that there's absolutely no room for error. For example, what would happen if in July customers A and D don't actually pay their bills and can't pay until September or October. That takes $29,900 of revenue out of July and shifts it out two or three months. The business would immediately exhaust its line of credit and wouldn't be able to pay its bills. Without enough cash on hand, this could spell disaster for Newco. We'd suggest either raising more capital to start, or planning for an additional infusion of outside capital sometime in May. Or, the founder of Newco could revisit the expense projections to make sure that all expenses as planned are indeed necessary—perhaps spending could be reduced to make cash last longer.

The takeaway? In business as in life, it's fair to expect the unexpected. No matter how tightly you plan the first year in business, in the real world there will inevitably be variations in the amount—and timing—of revenues and expenditures. How sensitive to these variations will your business be? If your cash management report suggests that you're as vulnerable as Newco, you might want to add a bit more cushion for security. And once you start up, make sure you review the cash management report regularly. Include a column for "variance" so you can see whether you're performing better or worse than projected and adjust your plans accordingly.

Making the Perfect Pitch

If you're contracted to raise money for your business, once you've gotten your business plan together, it's time to condense it into an "elevator pitch" that you can use at the spur of the moment. We give entrepreneurs the chance to practice their elevator pitch on StartupNation Radio every week. The name comes from that "once-in-a-lifetime" opportunity. You step onto the elevator at the first floor, and who steps on right behind you? The financier of your dreams—the one you've been trying to get a meeting with for months.

You've got a 60-second ride to hook the investor's interest before the doors open and he steps out of your life forever. This is your shot to really test how well you can explain your business and its vision. It might seem insignificant, but it's crucial to be able to get to the heart of your idea instantaneously and engage the interest of the money people. The perfect elevator pitch shows that you understand your business so well that you can simply and succinctly tell anyone exactly what it is in 60 seconds flat. You'll be amazed at how often you'll find yourself using your perfect pitch.

To prepare yourself, write down the answers to these 10 questions:

1. *What's the idea?* Have that on the tip of your tongue. It's your leadoff.
2. *What's the status of your idea?* One or two sentences only! Mention patent status if that pertains. And stage of development.
3. *What market need does your idea address?* Investors get excited about businesses that address what's called a "screaming need." Describe that need with a one-liner.
4. *What feedback do you have indicating you're onto something hot?* Refer to a testimonial if you've got one. If you don't have one, *get one!*
5. *How are you going to get people to buy what you offer?* Mention your brilliant marketing and distribution strategy that distinguishes you from the competition.

6. *What's special about you or your team?* Put a lot of emphasis on team qualifications. As we always say, a great team can make even an average idea into a winner, but an average team has tough odds no matter how incredible the idea is.

7. *What's the total funding you're seeking?* Throw out a number. You're a passionate entrepreneur and *you're on a mission!*

8. *What's the fund-raising strategy?* To show you understand investors' needs in general, give a highlight of some deal terms, just enough to show off your savvy and sensitivity to investor objectives.

9. *What's the projected return on investment?* Give a taste of the magnitude of the success you expect and the winnings the investor will enjoy.

10. *What's next?* Finish strong with a specific question like "Can I walk you through my business plan—it really outlines how big this opportunity is."

We know it's possible to hit all of these points in a compelling way because we've received many hundreds of elevator pitches on StartupNation Radio and in our role as venture capitalists. To do this right, you have to write out your script, rehearse it over and over, and totally memorize it. One trick is to time yourself while you leave a message on your own voice mail. Then listen to your pitch and critique yourself!

FAST FACT: PLAY TO YOUR AUDIENCE

Have you ever watched QVC? The people who are on the screen hawking the products are actually being coached while you watch. When they say something on air and it causes viewers to start dialing in like mad, the director immediately gets word to the on-air people advising them to hammer on the point that's causing a positive response.

You have to do the same thing in your elevator pitch.

And think on your feet. If you find yourself delivering a pitch and the investor reacts in a particularly positive way to a point you just made, then dwell on that a little bit. *You're looking for the hot buttons.* When you find those buttons, *keep pushing!*

To review a full archive of elevator pitches from StartupNation Radio, click on www.startupnation.com/elevatorpitch.

Living with Your Business Plan

Your business plan should be created once and then re-created many times over in the years to come. It should truly be a living, dynamic document that evolves as you and the market evolve together.

One thing we are often asked is "Should I stick to my business plan no matter what happens?" There are no hard-and-fast rules on changing or updating business plans. But one rule of thumb we use is "Listen to the market."

The behavior and feedback of your customers, whoever they may be, will help tell you whether you're on target or if you need to revisit your plan. They'll either want what you have, the way you offer it, and will pay the price you sell it for, or they won't. If that's the case, you've got to either adjust the plan to accommodate the target market or change the target market to better fit what you're offering.

Meet Todd Graham and Jonathan Hudson, two entrepreneurs who sidestepped their last years of University of Michigan schooling to cofound their dream business. As college students during the Napster file-swapping controversy of the early 2000s, they came up with an idea to create software to protect audio files from being sent around the Internet without permission. They created a business plan to target the music industry.

But as they got more and more feedback from the marketplace, the two entrepreneurs learned that there was an even more appealing target market—and they retooled their marketing focus in the plan completely. They realized that the best customer for their innovative technology was not the music industry at all. Instead, today their company, Indigo Security, produces security software to control access to digital information inside major companies. Law firms, banks, and other major customers have signed on as initial customers, but that's just the tip of the iceberg for Indigo. The market they're going after is estimated to incur over $80 billion in loss of proprietary information *each year*.

Had they not taken the time to test their business plan in the marketplace, they would have squandered a very exciting technology in an area where it didn't fit best.

On the flipside, take the story of Patrick Byrne, founder of Overstock.com.

STICKING TO STRATEGY: OVERSTOCK.COM

Patrick Byrne, the founder of Overstock.com, started with a business plan that was downright unpopular with potential investors. He stuck to it, however, and ended up on top. Patrick shopped his idea for an online version of the discount mall to several dozen venture capitalists during the dot-com boom of the late 1990s. Not one of the 55 firms he approached would give him the time of day. They told the Stanford grad and former executive with Warren Buffett's Berkshire Hathaway that his proposal "was a dumb business idea."

His plan? Buy the closeouts and surplus goods of major manufacturers and sell them at bargain-basement prices at his online store, Overstock.com. The venture capitalists pooh-poohed this idea, but Patrick believed in his business plan. More important, as he told us in 2003, he believed in his customers. "I never once thought about changing my business plan, because I could tell from my customers that I was right."

(continued on next page)

Left with no other funding options, Patrick decided to go it alone and financed the company himself through his own savings. He even took the company public through a Dutch auction, much like the one Google used to go public in 2004, giving many Main Street investors the opportunity to buy stock in his Salt Lake City company.

Five years after the last venture capitalist turned him down, Byrne has seven million customers coming to his site every month, expects to be profitable in 2005, and employs 400 people in the Salt Lake suburb of Cottonwood Heights. And although Patrick says he's not one to gloat, Overstock.com has helped liquidate many of the now-defunct dot-coms that venture capitalists chose to finance over his company, selling off their office furniture, computers, and servers for a profit. Not bad for a business plan that was once called "dumb."

Patrick stuck to his business plan because his customers were telling him they liked what he had to offer. He listened to the market, and now Overstock.com has more than seven million shoppers a month and ranks with Target.com and BestBuy.com as one of the Internet's favorite shopping sites.

To Inc or Not to Inc? A Little Structure Goes a Long Way

Is an LLC—a limited liability company—the right choice for you, or is it better to create a corporation? Is it best to simply operate as a sole proprietorship? What's the difference between an S and a C corporation?

The answers to these questions lie in the specifics associated with your business. To determine the best structure, you need to understand the advantages and disadvantages of each. Then, by using your business plan, match up your objectives with the one that's right for you. To ensure that you're considering all the appropriate variables, answer the following questions:

- Does your plan call for equity investors?
- Will you have more than one class of shareholder?
- Do you plan to take your company public?
- Do you want to maintain control over the company as other investors become involved?
- Do you anticipate losses that can be passed along as a tax advantage in the early going?
- Do you want to avoid double taxation?
- Is there a significant risk of liability associated with your specific business?

Think through these critical issues carefully. Your answers will help guide you to the right business structure and steer you away from the wrong ones. Each structure has its own quirks, upsides, downsides, and tax implications.

Sole Proprietorships

Operating as a sole proprietor means you operate your business without forming a separate entity. It's the most common form of business organization. You can file a "doing business as" ("dba") form with the state and open a bank account using your personal Social Security number instead of a federal tax ID number. The profits and losses from the business are accounted for on your personal tax return instead of through a company tax return. By operating as a sole proprietor, you save on the expense associated with filing and maintaining a separate entity such as a corporation or an LLC.

This type of entity is a common choice for anyone operating a business where there are no investors or partners and when there's

> **QUICK TIP**
>
> You can file for incorporation or other company structures at the Secretary of State's office or the Corporations Commission in your state. Check your government listings. The costs vary per state, but the fees are generally around $50. If you're not sure which structure is best, we recommend consulting with your attorney or accountant for help in determining the best structure for you.
>
> As an alternative, you can contract with a company that specializes in corporate and LLC filings to do this work.

little liability exposure. Let's say, for example, you're an independent graphic designer or you want to start a home-based eBay business. A sole proprietorship would be a perfectly suitable way to go. The key consideration when choosing the sole proprietorship form is the issue of personal-liability exposure. Should anyone take action against your company for any reason, your personal assets would be exposed. One way to mitigate the liability concern is to take out a personal-liability umbrella policy as a measure of safety. Jeffrey Weiss, Esq., of Jaffe, Raitt, Heuer & Weiss, P.C., an experienced, no-nonsense lawyer we've grown to trust over the years, has a piece of wisdom about the risks you assume in a sole proprietorship. "While operating as a sole proprietor for the first year can be an easy, cost-effective way to be in business without incurring any extra expenses associated with a corporation or LLC, I believe you have to think long and hard about the choice to operate as a sole proprietor given the potential liability risks. It's so simple and relatively cheap to form an entity such as an LLC, I almost always think it's a better choice," he says.

Nonetheless, sole proprietorships remain the single most widely used form of business in America. It's up to you to decide which works best. Consider these pros and cons:

Sole Proprietorships

Upside ↑

- Easy to start, simple to maintain
- Low-cost way to operate
- No double-taxation issues
- Owner has complete managerial control

Downside ↓

- Personal-liability exposure
- All responsibilities are on single owner
- Only one owner is allowed

Partnerships

This type of structure is commonly used when two or more people agree to operate as a business. Both you and your partner(s) are considered business owners who contribute time, money, skills, and other things in order to share business profits, assets, and losses. The individual partners create a separate entity called a "partnership." This type of entity avoids the burden of additional taxation found in other structures you'll learn about. Profits and losses are "passed through" to the individuals in the partnership and reflected on each individual's personal tax return. Businesses operating as partnerships need to be sensitive to the issue of liability exposure for the owners. In a general partnership, each owner is individually liable.

In a special partnership called "limited partnerships," you can have two classes of owners. The first is the "general partners," the entrepreneurs who operate the partnership and as a result have liability exposure. The second type of partner in a limited partnership is a "limited partner," such as an investor. Limited partners have no day-to-day involvement in the operations of the business, and generally have no liability exposure.

"For similar reasons to the sole proprietorship, a partnership is not a preferred choice of entity either," according to Jeff Weiss. "The partners are completely liable for all the obligations of the partnership, so there's no limitation of liability, and there's simply too much exposure."

Here are some of the pros and cons for partnerships:

QUICK TIP

With this structure, given that you'll assume personal liability, it's important to know your partner very well and to be confident in his/her character and commitment. Ask yourself: How much do I trust my partner? How aligned are my partner's goals relative to mine?

Your partner's decisions for the business can impact you personally, so make sure you have no doubts that you can work together.

> ## PARTNERSHIPS
>
> ### Upside ↑
>
> - Allows for pass-through of profits and losses to owners; no double taxation
> - Allows for multiple owners, both active and passive
> - General partners have complete managerial control
> - Provides liability protection for passive owners
>
> ### Downside ↓
>
> - Personal-liability exposure for general partners
> - More costly than a sole proprietorship

Corporations

A corporation comes in two basic forms—a C corporation and an S corporation. Each type is formed as a separate entity and the owners in either type, known as "shareholders," can be active or passive in the activities of the company. As a general matter, the shareholders are not responsible for fees, liabilities, or losses associated with the business.

The basic difference between the two types is that the S corporation allows for a pass-through of the profits and losses to the shareholders—similar to a partnership format—while the C corporation is taxed at both the corporate level and the shareholder level. Virtually all publicly traded companies are C corporations. The stock, money, and assets earned by the corporation belong to the corporation. Dividends are distributed to shareholders under the direction of the corporation's shareholder-elected board of directors. Stockholders then pay taxes on the earned dividends, and the corporation also pays taxes on all profits, known as "double taxation." While S corporations offer tax advantages to their shareholders, S corporations are not very flexible because they must adhere to certain limitations dictated by the Internal Revenue

Code, such as the total number and type of shareholders they can have. Further, S corporations can issue only one class of stock.

To become incorporated, you fill out the appropriate documents for the state where your business will be based, and you have all shareholders vote on overall corporate management, stock shares, name of the company, business purpose, and other key aspects pertaining to the business.

Note that you'll need to hold annual stockholder meetings and keep meticulous records to avoid legal and accounting problems. Forming a corporation is an intricate process, so, as is the case with all of these structures, we highly recommend that you consult an attorney.

CORPORATIONS

Upside ↑

- Well known and understood by many
- Low risk of liability
- Can sell stock to investors in order to raise money

Downside ↓

- Expensive to form and maintain
- Must be detailed and meticulous in accounting, taxation, and reporting matters
- Shareholders in C corporations encounter double taxation

Limited Liability Companies

The LLC business structure is a relatively new type of entity that's quickly becoming one of the most popular, and for good reason. The LLC combines the qualities of a corporation with those of a limited partnership. Like a corporation, an LLC is a separate legal entity, so the owners are not responsible for the debts and liabilities of the company, but like a partnership, profits and losses can be passed through to the owners, known as "members," so double taxation can be avoided. The members pay taxes on their distribution of the LLC's profits through their individual tax returns. In addition to the tax and liability advantages, Jeff Weiss says the LLC structure is his preferred choice of entity because "It offers unlimited flexibility in the number and type of members as well as the classes of equity interests." This gives you options you may want as your business grows.

One of the best things about an LLC is that control over the entity is not tied to the percentage of ownership each member has. This provides great flexibility if investors are to be involved. You could sell a majority of the company to investors yet still maintain control.

Note one caveat: If you're planning to raise venture capital or eventually do a public offering as an exit strategy, you may need to convert the LLC to a corporation. Depending on the particular circumstances, this conversion may be completed relatively easily without major tax implications.

LIMITED LIABILITY COMPANIES

Upside ↑

- Low risk of liability
- No double taxation
- Can have multiple owners, both active and passive

Downside ↓

- Not as widely known and understood as corporations or partnerships
- Not best vehicle for raising venture capital or going public
- More expensive to operate than a sole proprietorship
- Not yet recognized in all states (e.g., Texas).

Our Bottom Line

No matter how simple your idea may seem at the outset, you can't skip the business-planning process we've laid out. Whether you're going to be an LLC or sole proprietorship, whether you'll work from home or employ dozens from your brick-and-mortar location, whether you're going to fund the business yourself or through investors—*you absolutely must create a business plan.* Researching, crafting, and using this plan will help you know the right moves to make and when to make them.

Perhaps most important, the business plan is an outgrowth of your Life Plan. It's a vehicle that delivers you closer to what's important to you personally. It's the dictate that wields the power to impact and transform the lives of your customers, your employees, your financiers, and, most important, you.

Building a Healthy Business

Fresh Baby, LLC

Vital Stats

- Year Founded: 2002
- 2004 Revenue: $300,000
- No. of Employees: 2
- Headquarters: Virtual
- For Radio Interview: www.startupnation.com/book

Big Idea

Create a business based on a family tradition of making home-made baby food and market the system as an answer to the childhood obesity epidemic.

We featured Cheryl Tallman on our radio show in April of 2003. She embodied so much of what we believe in—leaving the corporate hierarchy behind, dreaming up an idea, and then pursuing it. She now runs a business from home, outsourcing operations to reliable vendors, and commercializing a product that could do a lot of good in the world.

SLOAN BROTHERS: Hewlett Packard was born in a garage. Was your business born in the kitchen?

CHERYL: It was born in the kitchen. Actually, I started the company with my sister, who's a mother of four, and I'm a mother of one.

SLOAN BROTHERS: So you have a focus group of five available to you at any time?!

CHERYL: Exactly, five fresh babies.

Cheryl Tallman never thought she'd be selling products that help consumers make their own fresh baby food for a living. For most of her professional life, she'd been a hard-charging executive running her own New York–based marketing firm, TSM. But in 2000, she sold the business, had a baby, and decided to move with her husband from Manhattan to the idyllic little town of Petoskey on the north shore of Lake Michigan.

One day, as she was trying to wean her son Spencer off of formula and switch him to real food, she opened up a bottle of peas. She was so revolted by the smell that she threw them away, thinking they were spoiled. When the next bottle smelled exactly the same way, she called her mom for advice. Her mom simply explained that a lot of mass-produced bottled baby food smelled that way. "It's the preservatives," Cheryl's mom informed her. In a quandary over what to feed Spencer, she called her sister, Joan Ahlers, who had raised her four children on homemade baby food. Joan sent her a care package with a blender, recipes, and instructions on how to make and freeze baby food. That's when Cheryl realized there might just be a business idea inside that care package. Perhaps she could duplicate the package and sell it as a kit—with recipes, instructions, and useful storage containers.

But it wasn't until Cheryl began to research the baby food industry that she happened onto the key marketing message that would turn her concept from a cute idea into a powerful brand, the type we call a "marching brand." No, that's not a typo—we define marching brands as those that are consistent, immediately recognizable, and deliver a clear and compelling message.

With childhood obesity reaching epidemic proportions, Cheryl decided to pitch her brand and products as a quick, easy, and inexpensive way to instill good eating habits in children and thereby cut down on obesity. She decided to focus her brand building on health care professionals, the people new parents often turn to first for advice. Instead of introducing yet another baby food to the crowded category, Cheryl created a do-it-yourself product that is now recommended by thousands of pediatricians, midwives, and other child care practitioners.

Listening to Cheryl's story, Fresh Baby seems like such a simple, smart idea, but in hindsight, remedying the problem of childhood obesity with products for making fresh, homemade baby food seems like pure genius.

Like so many of the great ideas we hear from entrepreneurs, Cheryl could have taken her business in several different directions. She could have made organic, preservative-free baby food and sold it like Diane Keaton did in the film *Baby Boom*, creating a consumer-focused brand with a big advertising budget to drive new mothers to her products. But as we learned from our chats with Cheryl, the obvious choices weren't necessarily the best choices, as she discovered through her process of "getting real" about her idea. As we listened to Cheryl, we were impressed with just how in-depth and diligent she was with her "getting real" process, one that we espouse for any small-business entrepreneur. Cheryl's story illustrates how doing your homework and making savvy choices early on can set the tone for your entire business—

from the brand positioning to how you organize your company.

Cheryl didn't really start thinking seriously about fresh baby-food-making products as a business idea until she was chatting with a former colleague about what she was going to do with the rest of her life, now that she had sold her marketing business and had started a family. Again, this informal type of "vetting" process can be a very important step in figuring out if the kernel of an idea you have actually has some commercial potential. "I started telling her about making fresh baby food. I went on and on about how cost-effective it was to make your own baby food, how easy, how economical, and how nutritional. My friend finally butted in to my stream of consciousness and said, 'Cheryl, you sound just like an infomercial for this. Why isn't this the next step in your life?'"

That chat was Cheryl's first big *ah-hah!* moment, the moment when she realized she really did have a business and not just a wacky idea.

What Cheryl did next couldn't please us more. She sat down to write a business plan. Truthfully, many successful small businesses have started without ever having a business plan. But Cheryl knew, probably more than most business owners, that she had to find out if there was even a market for her idea, and if there was, who was the competition? She also wanted to put it in writing so she could persuade her sister, Joan, to become her business partner. "I knew I couldn't do this without her," Cheryl says with conviction, which reminded us of our decision to work together on the Battery Buddy.

Cheryl is straightforward about how important it is to understand your market potential and your competition: "When you're starting out, there's a part of you that really doesn't want to know if somebody else is doing it. You don't want somebody to poke a hole in your dream. You'd rather stick your head in the sand and just go for it. But you're really kidding yourself if you think you're the first person who has thought of this idea. There's always going to be a competitor out there. What you really need to figure out is how to get your butt in front of consumers."

We couldn't have said it better or more bluntly: Doing your homework by scouring the market for competitors is imperative, no matter how much you want to avoid it at first. You'll find as Cheryl did that an in-depth, competitive analysis can actually confirm your idea and then help craft the perfect positioning for your company.

Here's what Cheryl found as she researched competitors and consumers.

She took copious notes about the boom in organic and natural products, especially in children's food products. Beech-Nut, Gerber, and others already had a line of healthier bottled baby foods on the market. Producing her own brand didn't feel like much of an option. But four million babies are born every year in the United States; if she could reach even a tenth of that market, she knew she'd have a continually replenishing market for her product.

Those two pieces of research helped her hone her idea for marketing a do-it-yourself fresh-baby-food-kit company. With a market of four million babies, she knew lots of other companies had thought about natural, organic, and fresh baby food. The key was to find a new angle. It wasn't until she started reading the daily newspapers that it finally hit her. "The constant drumbeat of stories about the childhood obesity problem reminded me of when tobacco and tobacco-related deaths became a huge story," she said. Cheryl began researching companies such as Nicoderm and nicotine-gum companies, as well as natural tobacco companies that started up during that time. She paid particular attention to how much media attention these companies received when they pitched themselves as a healthier or safer alternative to smoking. Cheryl had her "idea epiphany" at that point. "I just knew this same kind of attention would be paid to companies that could do something about this obesity epidemic. I knew then that I could get media attention for my company if I focused on that niche. That would help me build brand equity without having to compete with the big ad budgets of a competitor such as Gerber."

Unlike Gerber, however, Cheryl didn't yet have an actual brand name to work with. "I know now it sounds pretty funny. I'd been shopping this business plan around and doing all this research, and I'd never named the company," Cheryl laughingly recalls to us. While she spent months researching the competition and the market, Cheryl spent just 30 seconds talking to her husband about the name of the company. "It was sort of serendipity. My husband wondered what I was going to name this company, and I thought about [my son] Spencer. I was always calling him fresh baby because he was so precocious. It was perfect."

Cheryl's story illustrates that what's really important in creating a "marching brand" is your brand's positioning.

She set out to spread the word about her product through any means possible. She began writing a book with her sister about their experiences making fresh baby food. She started pitching her ideas to the press about how homemade baby food could aid in the childhood obesity epidemic. "In our first year, we were mentioned 75 times in the press, including big national magazines like *Organic Style*," Cheryl says. That kind of press attention can't be bought; it's a smart way for businesses to build awareness without spending a lot of money.

She made a list of all the medical and child care conventions she needed to go to. At the top of the list was the American Academy of Pediatrics conference. "We set up a booth there and started handing out free patient information to the doctors. We tried to be more educational and informational than anyone else."

They searched for new places and opportunities to reach out to parents through health care professionals. "We realized early on in this venture that parents no longer depend on pediatricians for advice about the health of their children. People have all kinds of lifelines. They use childbirth experts, lactation consultants, and midwives. People in these roles have become trusted advisors, so we go to their conferences as well. They like it because nobody pays attention to them. But we do, and what's great is it helps our marketing. They've offered us some invaluable advice that's helped create new products for our company."

A year ago, a lactation consultant suggested that they might want to create a product for mothers who are breast-feeding. "Many mothers just store the milk in plastic bags. They don't know how much milk is in the bag, so they often end up wasting a lot," Cheryl explains. After consulting with the lactation expert, Fresh Baby developed a breast-milk freezer tray. Each cube is exactly one ounce, and there's a cover to keep it safe from smells and spills. "Each time you need milk, you just pop out how many ounces you need."

Such an intense commitment to understanding how to market and sell Fresh Baby has helped Cheryl and Joan turn the company into a Super Startup in just two years. Sales jumped from $100,000 in 2003 to $300,000 in 2004, and Cheryl expects that same exponential growth as Fresh Baby gains distribution through powerhouse retailers such as Whole Foods.

But there's one other important lesson we learned from Fresh Baby, and it's tied, again, to this concept of *expertise*. Both sisters are quick to admit that their real strengths are in marketing and sales. For everything else—such as manufacturing and bookkeeping—they outsource. "In a small business, you find that you need to be an expert in so many things. I realized early on that I was never going to be an expert in accounting or warehouse management and it was simpler and more efficient to hire an expert," Cheryl says.

Outsourcing those types of back-office functions also means that Cheryl and Joan can continue to live the kind of lives they want even as they run what could become a multimillion-dollar business. Cheryl works from Petoskey, Michigan, and Joan continues to live in Los Alamos, New Mexico. The business is run primarily online, with manufacturing outsourced to a plant in Connecticut, and accounting done in Petoskey.

Cheryl's Key Moves:

1. **Business Planning.** Cheryl's research kept her from making mistakes like launching a sizable advertising campaign when she could better stir up demand by low-cost public relations. Using "grassroots marketing," she took her brand directly to the people who could make a difference: child care professionals who can have a huge impact on what new parents buy for their children.

2. **Outsourcing.** Fresh Baby is the quintessential virtual company, a trend that we applaud. Cheryl works just minutes from her home in a rented office in Petoskey. She handles all the marketing for the company, while her sister Joan handles sales. They outsource literally everything else, including accounting, logistics, warehousing, and manufacturing.

3. **Creating a Marching Brand.** Cheryl's way of turning Fresh Baby into a "marching brand" was extremely smart. She researched the market before she jumped into the business. She understood who her audience was and what her message was going to be so well that she could immediately target her marketing resources. This kind of understanding is crucial, since a marching brand is created through consistency in marketing efforts.

   She refined her message, as well. Linking Fresh Baby to childhood obesity was a key move. This connection not only gave her brand a difference, but it put her in the perfect position to pitch her brand through public relations.

Creating Your Own
Marching Brand

Think "Volvo," and you think safety. Think "Weight Watchers," and you think weight loss. Think "Rolex," and you think prestige. These are brands—each representing carefully chosen ideals and creating an identity for a product or company. What makes each of these brands a *marching brand* is that they're consistent, immediately recognizable, and deliver a clear and compelling message.

Choosing a Brand Name

We drew heavily upon the smarts of Stephanie Jacobson to guide you through a discussion about the importance of branding. Stephanie is our communications director and brand manager. More than anything, she's one of those superstar people you'll learn about in Chapter Seven—the kind of person who can take your business to a whole new level.

To get started, first identify your brand attributes—characteristics that strongly conjure up an impression of what makes your business unique and distinct. It could be words like "Friendly," "Smart," "Reasonably Priced," etc. Next, make a list of the demographic profile of the people who are your ideal customers. From a marketing and brand-building perspective, it's essential to understand the following about your target audience:

- Age range
- Location (local, regional, or national)
- Gender
- Income range
- Education level

- Ethnicity
- Preferred media (examples are print, broadcast, online)

Using the brand attributes and demographics you lay out for your business, it's time to get creative! It's likely you'll come up with a variety of names for your business. As you narrow the list to a favorite name, just be sure to check one thing: availability. Do a search to be sure some other business hasn't already taken it. If your budget is too thin to hire an intellectual property attorney, then conduct a search online on your own at the United States Patent and Trademark Office website (www.uspto.gov).

Consistency, Consistency, Consistency

When we're building a new company, it's always our objective to create a consistent look and feel for the company's logo and marketing materials. Think of Starbucks Coffee Company. It's no coincidence that on every printed item—from brochures, to coffee packaging, to catalogues, to your Starbucks Card—the green emblem always appears. This consistent reinforcement of the Starbucks brand is present in their coffee shops throughout the world, going beyond their perfectly foamed cappuccinos to elements such as furniture and music.

You should bring your brand to life through your employees as well. Give them a written document that describes the brand values of your company. When they interact with customers, they'll be equipped to express the ideals and priorities of your business in a consistent way.

Logo Development

A logo is the artistic embodiment of a brand. If you design your logo right, it will carry your brand through the life cycle of your business. Once you've identified your brand name and attributes, your graphic designer will have a better chance of building your brand's personality into a great logo. And color matters. For example, blue, used in many corporate logos, conjures up stability, red represents power, and brown stands for steadfast and dependable.

Creating a logo can be expensive. The fees charged by graphic designers are often based on the enduring value the logo will have, not necessarily on the time spent developing it. It's possible, however, to find extremely talented freelance graphic designers who are willing to charge you a reasonable hourly rate and who'll create just the logo you're looking for.

You might also choose to use a "tagline" to accompany your logo to further describe your product or service or possibly your brand values. When you start your business, don't get hung up on developing your permanent tagline right away. As your business gets under way, it'll become obvious what themes and language you want to include in a tagline, if you want one at all.

Creating a Website

Most modern businesses have some sort of website presence. Some companies' websites are used as nothing more than an online brochure. For other companies, the website *is* the company.

When possible, create a website address that's consistent with your brand. Ideally, the website address should simply be your brand name. For instance, StartupNation uses www.startupnation.com, which makes it easy for people to remember and to find. To conduct a search and to secure a website address, you can use online search and registration services such as www.register.com and www.networksolutions.com.

Your business objectives should dictate the extent of design and the functionality of your website. We recommend consulting with an experienced firm or freelancer whose business it is to develop

QUICK TIP

Know What to Ask

When you interview potential website developers be aware that website development costs fall into three categories: design, programming, and maintenance.

Get answers to the following questions:

- What will the costs be to maintain and update the site? Who'll do this?
- Where will the site be hosted? Will there be a monthly server cost?
- Will the site need e-commerce capabilities?
- Will the site be optimized for search engines?

websites. Ask to see their work before engaging them, and make sure their style is in sync with your business and brand. It's always smart to ask them for a written proposal that includes specifications for the project. And it never hurts to get more than one bid.

How to Create Demand for Your Brand

Before you "go live" with your startup, you should have a clear idea of how you're going to create awareness and demand. It's important to make sure you've got a marketing plan that outlines the priorities, strategies, schedule, and budget required to stir up that demand. Recognize that traditional forms of marketing such as paid advertising in print, online, outdoor, and broadcast mediums can be exceedingly expensive. If you're determined to use paid advertising to create demand, be sure to be very targeted with your ad dollars, and be prepared to advertise over an extended period of time before you see measurable results. In contrast, grassroots efforts can be more affordable, drawing mostly on your creativity and energy rather than your pocketbook.

Grassroots marketing is ideal for startups. It's a great way to achieve your marketing objectives without having to spend too much of your startup capital. Grassroots marketing gets its name from the place where this form of marketing starts—at the ground level, often involving one-on-one communication with members of your target market. Razor Scooters, all the rage in the late 1990s, became popular through a concerted grassroots campaign led by Razor's founder, Carlton Calvin.

"We never spent a single dollar on traditional advertising. It was all grassroots marketing and word of mouth that drove the demand," Carlton said proudly on StartupNation Radio. He got his scooters in the hands of the "cool kids" whenever he could. Excited about their new toy, the kids would immediately head outside to the sidewalks. With the Razor logo emblazoned on the scooters, wide-eyed kids looking on cried out, "I want one of those!" And demand spiked instantly. By strategically giving scooters to "influencers" in various communities, Carlton has sold five million Razor Scooters in just a few short years.

Here are some other ways that you can fertilize your grassroots marketing efforts:

- **The Power of PR:** In contrast to advertising, public relations generates editorial coverage of your business that you *don't* pay for. This kind of coverage—whether in print, in broadcast, or online—can be priceless. It presents information about who you are and what your business offers from a third-party perspective, and that adds credibility. You can leverage the coverage by having reprints made—with permission—and include them in your sales materials. To get your story picked up in the press, identify key media outlets and submit story ideas and/or opinion editorials on a subject. Get to know a reporter who's covering your beat, maybe over lunch. Write a press release announcing your new business and distribute it to targeted media contacts.

- **Speaking Up.** Research the events in your market niche and find out if you can get yourself on the agenda as a speaker. Positioning yourself as an expert goes a long way to landing financing, future partners, free coverage in the press, and customers.

- **Promotions in Motion:** Depending on what type of business you're starting, there may be promotions you can run to grab the attention of your target market. Make sure you have the right plan in place to create sufficient interest in the promotion. Consider using a free giveaway, discounts, or some other stunt to get the response you need.

- **Direct Mail:** Send out a postcard to all your contacts announcing your new business. You might send the postcard in an odd size or color—do whatever it takes to grab attention.

QUICK TIP

Keep Them Coming Back

Once someone visits your site, your next challenge is to get them to return. Brian Cleveland, our web master at startupnation.com, suggests that you update your website content frequently. Refresh your merchandise. Create a promotion and post it. Provide a new article. Add the latest news. Perhaps create a "blog,"—an online journal that people will want to read each day.

- **E-Mail Communications:** Start collecting e-mail addresses from the get-go. If you attend events, ask people you meet if you can place them on your e-mail list. As a convenient way to remember who gives you permission, make a mark on their business card. E-mail correspondence is a very cost-effective marketing tool—the costs are limited mostly to the set up. Be sure to obey privacy and spam laws, which may vary from state to state.

- **Networking:** Join associations important to your business, such as a local chamber of commerce or a trade group in your industry. Meet and talk with as many people as you can and keep in touch with them. They can form an invaluable network for you. Attend events and conferences to keep you in contact with your community and on the cutting edge of market trends.

Search Engine Marketing is another important marketing tool. Have you ever noticed that certain websites always seem to come up when you search for a product or service? It's not a coincidence—it's the result of search engine advertising, or "SEA." You can pay to place text ads alongside the normal search results on popular search engines such as Google, Yahoo!, and MSN. Recent statistics show that the majority of people don't know the difference between genuine search results and paid placement search results.

Here's how it works: advertisers place bids on different combinations of keywords that your potential customers might enter into a search engine. Let's say you're selling high-quality travel photographs. If you purchase keywords such as "black and white photography" or "photography of Europe," and a potential customer types those words into a search engine, your text advertisement will appear in the results, usually on the right side of the page. SEA ensures that links to your website appear in plain view at the very moment when people are actively searching for what you are selling. The beauty is that you pay for this service only when someone actually clicks on your link, distinguishing SEA as a "pay for performance" model of advertising.

Additionally, we suggest you implement search engine optimization, or "SEO." This is the process of making your website easily accessible and highly relevant to search engines. The beauty about "hits" that result from SEO? Every click you get is free! SEO positions your website to appeal to the software that search engines use to locate and highlight applicable sites. To optimize your site for search engines, work with your website designer or developer to include targeted keywords throughout the content on your website. Integrate those keywords throughout the titles and body of your web pages. Also include those keywords in links you establish to *and* from your website. Be aware—if your keywords are stuck inside of graphics on your website, search engines likely won't pick them up, and you may lose potential hits.

You can learn more about these and other techniques by visiting resources such as www.searchenginewatch.com, www.clickz.com, and www.wordtracker.com. You could also attend conferences like Jupiter Media's Search Engine Strategies conferences (www.searchenginestrategies.com) and subscribe to the newsletter offered at www.searchenginelowdown.com. The search companies themselves also offer resources such as http://buzz.yahoo.com, http://inventory.overture.com, or http://adwords.google.com. And of course, there are many search engine marketing firms that offer specialized services to orchestrate your SEO and SEA campaign for a fee.

> **QUICK TIP**
>
> **Online Public Relations**
>
> Another way to enhance your search engine results is through online public relations. If you're able to incorporate keywords and links in your press releases and post the releases with online news services, your website has even greater chances of turning up during a search.

CHAPTER SIX

Finding the Funding That's "Just Right"

The Goldilocks Approach

When we started working on the Battery Buddy, we had an almost empty bank account. We didn't have access to venture capital. No line of credit. We'd never heard of angel investors. Little did we know that we were like the majority of people who start their own business. One in five companies on the Inc. 500 list was bankrolled with less than $5,000.

In fact, some of the most successful businesses in the United States were born with barely enough funding to get them through their first year. Both the Subway sandwich franchise and Dell Computer (which Michael Dell began from his college dorm room) were started with $1,000 in capital. And how's this for low-budget? Logo Athletic, a major supplier to the National Football League, was started with just $250 in the bank and a credit card limit of $1,000.

It's true. It's likely that you don't need millions of dollars to start up your business.

What you do need is a sound financial strategy that will set you up with enough money to launch the business and operate it until the business can support itself on incoming revenues.

The type and amount of funding you seek will impact your

business operations as well as your lifestyle. It's imperative that you take into account what your objectives are in your Life Plan as well as your business plan *before* securing the money. While there are many ways to finance a business, we've created a rationale for getting the money that suits your objectives best. It's an approach that's worked well for us and for the many entrepreneurs we've coached over the years.

We call it the "Goldilocks Approach," and it's all about finding the funding that's *just right* for you.

Remember Goldilocks? As she tasted the different porridges in the bears' empty house, she found one that was too hot, one that was too cold, and finally she found the one that was just right. It's that last one—the "just right" one—you're looking for when it comes to finding the money to start and grow your business.

How the Goldilocks Approach Works

Coming up with a strategy to get financing for your business shouldn't start out as a matter of *how much* money you need. Rather, you should first figure out *what* you need the money for and *when* you'll need it. Only then should you focus on how much is necessary. With that simple shift in thinking, you'll be able to apply the Goldilocks Approach to help you find the right money at just the right time.

In order to understand the money that's just right for you, answer these questions:

1. What do I need the money for?

You shouldn't have to guess about how to answer this question. It's all in your business plan. Based on the financial needs indicated in your plan, you should *already* have a clear understanding of what you need the money for. Use your plan to quantify the amount of financing required to fund the operations of your business while revenues are insufficient to cover your expenses. Your needs might be as simple as paying rent or buying a new computer. Or they can be as big and complex as buying manufacturing equipment and leasing a factory. Do you want to pay yourself a salary, or can you do without a paycheck for a year and pump the profits back into the business? Do you need that office space, or could you convert a room in your house until you're ready to expand? Are employees a must, or could you outsource many of the noncore functions in your business? Will you spend money on television advertising, or use word-of-mouth grassroots marketing efforts instead? Be sure to account for lifestyle requirements as well. For example, if it's a priority to ensure financial security for your family's needs, make sure you've secured enough capital to cover that objective.

Base your conclusions on a "worst-case scenario." Things always take longer and cost more than you think, so plan conservatively. Think hard about the critical investments you must make so your company can move toward profitability. Remember that while you'll want to keep your expenses low in the startup phase, don't be shy about making investments that'll clearly help you create value and drive your business forward.

In order to make the most of every dollar, you have to spend wisely. Sticking to your well-thought-out budget in your business plan and making sure you've got the fundamentals covered can mean the difference between success and failure. We've found that there's definitely an art to knowing which expenditures help your company grow and which ones are tangential or even damaging to your business.

We learned that lesson the hard way early in our careers. In the mid-1990s, we were working with a young entrepreneur to bring a new exercise device to market that would create an upper body workout while jogging. We were seeking initial funding for the company and found a group of investors who were willing to make a significant investment. It was decided to market the product through an infomercial, an extremely risky strategy, but one with potential for a high payoff.

Unfortunately, the infomercial effort fell right in line with the statistics and our bold strategy bombed. From that point forward, our focus became simply survival—we had to scramble just to pay the light bill. We learned that what you use the money for has to first address the absolute necessities as laid out in your business plan, and only then can you entertain high-risk allocations of your precious capital.

By contrast, we made the *right* decision in 1995 when we started Sloan Ventures, our venture development firm.

We had decided that to get the company off the ground we needed $1 million in startup capital. On the money-raising trail, we were able to get a meeting with one of the leading angel investors in the city. He totally "got it"—he loved our plan and connected with us and our potential. But when he got around to telling us his terms of investment, we were faced with a conundrum. The investor offered us $2 million instead of the $1 million we were after. That made us drool. However, in return, he wanted 51 percent ownership and ultimate control over the company. It was an enticing offer—an extra $1 million, which we could've dropped into our bank account. But we would've immediately lost control of our company, and we essentially would have found ourselves working for someone else. This was *not* part of our plan. We didn't have a clear idea of what we would do with that extra money, and for us, preserving our equity, maintaining control, and protecting our lifestyle objectives were much more important than the money.

After much soul-searching and applying the Goldilocks Approach, we called him up and told him, "Thanks, but no."

We wanted to start the business and run it our own way. We didn't have a specific need for $2 million—we had a clear need for $1 million to do what we wanted to do. And we certainly didn't want to give up control of our company.

We stuck to our guns in the face of that temptation, and we thank our lucky stars every day! Today, this investor has become a good friend. He acknowledges our foresight and discipline and has even invested side by side with us in other ventures.

2. When do I need the money?

Timing is a critical part of the Goldilocks Approach. Figure out when you need the money—whether it's all up front or spread out over months or years. Once again, your business plan should lay out the demands your business will have for additional financing over time. Refer to the chart below to understand the types of capital that are available and at what stage they are appropriate.

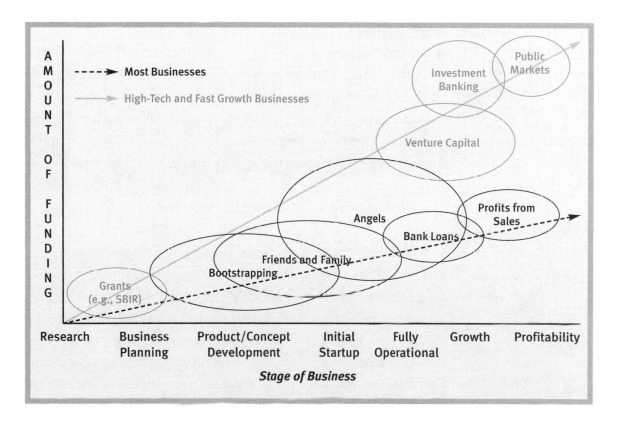

Notice in the chart how different sources of funding are appropriate for different stages of business. For example, you might want to go the route of Logo Athletic, which we mentioned earlier. They started out by bootstrapping and tapping credit cards. Later on, your ambition may grow and you may then need an infusion of capital to achieve your objectives—a bank loan or a "friends and family" investment. By planning ahead, you'll be able to create a strategy for funding throughout the life of the business. Create a timeline of when you'll need major infusions of cash and update it as your business grows.

Let's say you want to open a retail store. This scenario calls for an infusion of cash up front to rent or buy a space and initial inventory. You can do this through debt financing backed by the SBA, for example. Or you could get a loan from friends and family. As you'll learn later in this section, if the business needs more than $50,000 to get off the ground, you might want to consider angel investors.

Pay particular attention to your cash flow statement in the financial section of your business plan (see Chapter Five). You'll be able to see the periods of time when your revenues are not high enough to pay for the budget you've set up. That'll help you understand when your business will require infusions of capital from investors or lenders to supplement the shortfall.

3. How much money do I need?

When determining how much money you'll need for your business, refer back to the cash-flow projection outlined in the Financial Projections section of your business plan. Go back to the budget you prepared. Make sure you've been disciplined about allocating the money to activities that help you achieve your key milestones. Money is a precious resource, and you cannot afford to squander it. Every dollar counts. We're not suggesting you should be reluctant to spend money. Money is the fuel that makes a business grow. We're only suggesting you spend wisely and in accordance with a well-thought-out strategy as indicated in your business plan.

If you believe you've accounted for the most critical and the most necessary expenses in your forecasted budget, and if you believe your revenue projections are conservative and accurate, your cash flow projections will indicate when cash shortages will likely occur and by what amount. Make sure you'll have sufficient capital to help you get through these shortfalls.

With a clear understanding of the amount of capital you'll need, you're on your way to finding the funding that's neither too little or too much, too early or too late—you're positioned to find the funding that's just right!

Bootstrapping Your Startup

So you've figured out what you'll spend your money on, when you'll need it, and how much you'll require. Now it's time to talk about what kind of money is best for you. The first type of funding we'll cover is bootstrapping.

Bootstrapping relies on the sweat of your own hard work. Simply put, it's using your own money—or maybe running up some debt on credit cards—to start up your own company. We've used bootstrapping for several of our own businesses, and we hear from many entrepreneurs every week on our radio show and online who use this strategy as well. One of our favorites is the story of Phil LaDuca, who has bootstrapped—or "shoe-strapped"—his way to being a major provider of dance shoes to the likes of Renee Zellweger and Catherine Zeta-Jones.

Phil is a former Broadway dancer. He was an understudy for Gene Kelly in the original *Singin' in the Rain* and now works as a choreographer and dance teacher in New York City.

In November of 2000, he decided to take $20,000 of his own money to create an all-new dance shoe for professional dancers and sell it through a startup he called LaDuca Shoes. "The shoes had to be strong and supportive, but also needed to be flexible, something that was completely new in the industry," Phil told us on StartupNation Radio in 2003.

He opened a small store on Ninth Avenue in Manhattan in 2001, and started selling his shoes to dancers. He kept his day job teaching and choreographing to help pay the bills. With every sale he made, he turned right around and put the profits back into the business. He spent money creating a website so he could sell outside New York City, tapping new markets such as Las Vegas and Los Angeles. By using his contacts in the musical theater industry—instead of spending big money on advertising—he was able to get his shoes on the feet of the dancers in the film *Chicago*, including Zellweger and Zeta-Jones. How do you think Phil felt about his bootstrapping strategy as he watched *Chicago* for the first time, *his* shoes dancing across the screen?

Phil told us with great pride that he's been able to stay profitable and grow LaDuca Shoes by sticking to his narrow niche, all the while enjoying a lifestyle business that lets him keep doing what he loves—dancing. By 2004, Phil's original $20,000 investment had turned into $600,000 in sales—all from a little bit of bootstrapping.

Of course, there's a downside to this financing strategy. You have to be willing to do many things on a shoestring, like Phil's low-cost approach to bringing in new business—using his own contacts instead of big ad campaigns in dance publications. And you need to be willing to use your cash flow to help grow the business, instead of paying yourself a big salary. But in the long run, you may find that this bootstrap strategy will force you to be more disciplined than you may have been otherwise. And because you don't have to share the upside with investors, it'll entitle you to a far bigger portion of any profits. Again, it all comes down to

Goldilocks—what's the right money at the right time for your business? Depending upon your answer, bootstrapping may *not* be the best choice. You may have to tap into funds sooner or in greater amounts than what bootstrapping will provide. In that case, you'll have to go to an external source of financing.

Getting Money Without Giving Up Equity

D ebt financing. SBA loans. Friends and family. Angels. Venture capital. There's a variety of options available when seeking funding from others. Some forms of funding are provided in exchange for ownership; others aren't. Some want a degree of control over the business; others don't. Some invest in pure startups, while others invest capital for growth once the company's proven itself a winner. And remember, some types of financing are strictly for specific types of businesses. Just make sure you understand the differences when it comes to the type of financing you pursue.

Here's a breakdown of some of the most common.

Traditional Debt Financing

Debt financing is basically borrowing money that charges interest and must be repaid. Banks are the most common source to obtain debt financing, usually in the form of a traditional commercial loan.

In the past few decades, some banks have been reluctant to loan to small businesses because they saw them as more risky than lending to larger businesses and less profitable than personal loans such as home mortgages and car loans. Now more than ever, even the biggest banking conglomerates are turning their focus to small businesses as promising customers.

FAST FACT: LOANS

About eight million small-business loans, totaling $279 billion, were originated in 2003. Surprisingly, loans to companies with revenues under $1 million were larger on average—approximately $42,250—than loans to companies that generated more than $1 million—roughly $30,300.

Source: 2004 Fact Sheet—Federal Financial Institutions Examination Council (FFIEC) for institutions reporting under the Community Reinvestment Act (CRA) regulations.

To make the most of your opportunity, be prepared to build a solid case with the bank just as you would with any investor. Robert Bond, senior vice president and division manager of retail banking at Washington Mutual, offers the following crucial advice to help you land a bank loan on your first try.

"Banks like doing business with companies that already have a proven track record," Robert says. "But if you haven't owned a business before, make the most of your prior experience and successes. Highlight experiences that show you have what it takes to run a business."

If you're just starting out, you'll be asked for several years of tax returns and they'll want to do a check of your personal and business credit to see how you've handled debt in the past. "But don't let existing financials stand by themselves," Robert says. "You need to be prepared to show the bank your formal business plan. You need an income statement, a balance sheet, and a profit-and-loss statement."

Remember the bank is making an "investment" in you, Robert says, and that means the loan manager will want to see that you understand the financial side of your business. "You should know what your debt-to-income ratio is and what your debt-to-net-worth ratio is as well. This will help show the bank that you understand how much debt you can actually take on and pay back."

Be prepared to answer tough questions, such as "How risky is your business?" or "What will you do if the business doesn't bring in the kind of sales needed to pay back the loans?" These are questions you should ask yourself even before you set up that first appointment with a banker.

If you qualify, you and the bank have several options. If you need a quick infusion of cash—and your financials are solid—the bank may offer you a short-term commercial loan. Make certain you understand the terms. Short-term commercial loans often have higher interest rates and need to be paid back on an accelerated schedule. You may also be eligible for a line of credit. But again, check the interest rates and the terms of the credit line. Credit lines can help keep you liquid—providing you cash when you most need it—but they can come with fees.

Finally, the bank may decide on a long-term commercial loan that typically comes with lower rates and a repayment schedule that stretches over years, not months. No matter what type of loan you receive, Robert cautions you to understand the terms of the loan completely. "Always confirm with yourself and any of your business partners that you can pay back the loans through cash flow and have enough left over to continue running your business successfully." It's a good idea to factor in a small "cushion" of money in reserve in the event that your cash flow isn't as planned. This helps ensure you'll be able to always make that loan payment.

Whatever you do, don't take more money than you need. If you're a strong candidate, banks may tell you you qualify for more money than you're seeking. This can be tempting, but it can also send you off course. Stick to your business plan, and take the loan only in the amount you require. If you demonstrate perfect performance on that loan, you can always go back for more—and you can probably negotiate better loan terms.

If you don't qualify for a traditional loan, there's a viable option for you to consider. It's a loan backed by the Small Business Administration. This government agency provides a broad range of financial options that have helped the likes of FedEx and Intel get their start. The SBA guaranteed $12.5 billion in loans in 2004, more than in any previous year. While the average size of each loan guaranty was smaller on average than in previous years, this financing resource shouldn't be ignored.

Here's a quick look at what the SBA offers.

- 7(a) Loans: These loans can be used for working capital as well as for fixed assets. They're actually issued by banks but backed by a guaranty from the SBA. Remember, the SBA no longer loans money directly to individuals or businesses, but uses private financial institutions instead. To receive a 7(a) loan, businesses apply to a commercial financial institution, which then decides whether the application needs the SBA guaranty.

  To find a lender that works with the SBA in your community, check the financing link at www.sba.gov. Don't be turned off by common misperceptions that there's a lot of paperwork and government bureaucracy involved, and don't assume that a 7(a) loan only makes sense if you've been turned down by a bank already. "People believe that we are the lender of last resort," says Joseph Loddo with the SBA's district office in Washington, D.C. "But we're more like an insurance company for banks making small business loans than we are lenders to small businesses."

  Many of the SBA's applications are just one page long, according to Loddo, and in some SBA loan cases an application need only be submitted to the bank, not the SBA itself. Their turnaround times on guarantying a loan are within 48 hours, and most of them are guaranteed within 24 hours. You can visit www.startupnation.com and click on the Webinar Wednesday archives to view and listen to Joe Loddo's presentation on the various forms of SBA financing.

- 504 Loans: These loans are clearly earmarked for fixed assets such as land, buildings, or major pieces of equipment. You cannot use these loans for working capital, to repay debt, or to refinance. Rather, they're considered a long-term financing tool used by businesses and are provided to help drive economic development in a community. These loans are more complex, so you should read about them in detail on the SBA's website. But in brief, the loan includes a private-sector lender who puts in 50 percent of the capital to cover the project's cost. A Certified Development Company, a nonprofit corporation set up to drive economic development, puts up another 40 percent, which is backed by the SBA. Finally, the business seeking the financing is expected to contribute the last 10 percent of equity to the project.

BANK LOANS

Amount of Capital Available

- Varies greatly, depending on the size of the bank and the size and stage of your business

Upside ↑

- You don't have to give up equity
- Banks don't require control over your business

Downside ↓

- Banks are reluctant to lend to pure startups (except when the SBA provides a guaranty)
- Interest payments cut into cash flow and can reduce profits in the early stages
- May require a personal guaranty

Friends and Family

Friends and family are common sources of financing to turn to when starting a new business. After all, who knows you better? Who more than friends and family want to see you succeed? They

QUICK TIP

Get It in Writing

Even when getting a loan from a "friends and family" source, put the deal in writing and have both parties sign it. Making sure the details are understood and agreed upon keeps valued relationships healthy.

aren't going to require the same tough qualifications that banks will, and they'll probably provide the loan at the best terms available. Tempting, right? But be careful. When utilizing funds from friends or family to start a business, recognize that you could be putting your most valued relationships on the line. In order to mitigate the possibility of damaging your relationships, you must share your business plan. Go over your strategies and explain potential pitfalls. Let them know that their money's at risk. Further, we suggest that you treat the arrangement the same way you would treat a loan from a bank. Schedule regular payments just as you would if you were repaying a bank loan, and make sure you make them—on time. There is a temptation to get soft with a loan from friends and family, but you can easily get behind, the debt can pile up, and you'll be confronted with having to make a very uncomfortable explanation. The money is not a "gift" unless they tell you it is. Perhaps most important, frequent and straightforward communication is key. Friends and family will be most willing to be flexible on the repayment terms as long as you communicate the good news and the bad news, and set expectations accordingly.

FRIENDS AND FAMILY

Amount of Capital Available

- Generally less than $50,000

Upside ↑

- Will finance a startup
- Will say "Yes" when others say "No"
- Will likely offer best terms
- Will be more flexible if going gets tough

Downside ↓

- Be prepared to put your most valued relationships at risk
- Be ready for an ugly Thanksgiving dinner at your in-laws' if you lose their money

Using Your Equity to Raise Money

Equity financing is an exchange of funding for ownership. Tens of thousands of companies are funded each year by capital provided in exchange for equity. It's capital that's not required to be repaid as loans are. Instead, the investors receive a return on their investment in proportion to the percentage of their ownership. This occurs when distributions of profits are made or when the company is sold. Equity financing can come from high-net-worth private investors known as "angels," or from the most sophisticated of professional investors—venture capitalists. The amount of equity investors receive is based on the valuation of your company and the amount of capital they invest. For example, if you value your company at $1,000,000 and the investor puts up $250,000, then the investor receives 25 percent ownership in the company. For startup companies, the amount of equity to be awarded is more art than science. In the end, the right amount is determined largely by negotiation between you and the investor.

Angel Investors

Angel investors are people who've already made fortunes in their own businesses and who have money at their disposal to invest in other ventures. The Center for Venture Research estimates that 220,000 of these "angels" helped fund 42,000 businesses in 2003, with over $18 billion of investment. What's more, over 50 percent of angel investors' funds went into seed stage or startup companies. Angels earn their nickname by being known as friendly and patient about their investments. They are commonly willing to invest at an earlier stage, and they are willing to wait longer for a return on their investment than other equity-financing sources. For the most part, angels are the best equity-financing source to pursue if you're a pure startup. If one angel's not enough for your financing needs, you'll be glad to know that angels frequently like to invest with other angels. So once you involve one, it's likely that others will follow.

And angels often provide more than money.

In addition to their role as "money people," Angels often provide mentorship. They like to be tapped for their wisdom. They enjoy being in on the ground floor of innovative companies and contributing to their success. Angels like to take pride in the businesses in which they invest, something we call "psychic income." Oftentimes, angels act as a networking resource as well. They can introduce you to potential customers, strategic partners, and vendors they know well from their own business dealings. And as your financing needs grow beyond the means of what these individual investors are able to provide, angels can be indispensable in making introductions to later-stage financing sources.

ANGEL INVESTORS

Amount of Capital Available
- $25,000 to $1 million

Upside ↑
- Will invest in a pure startup
- Will invest for equity, avoiding drain on cash flow
- Will provide smarts and networking
- Will be relatively patient about the investment

Downside ↓
- It's often hard to get their attention
- You have to provide some portion of your equity
- You'll have to give up some measure of control
- You'll have to do formalized reporting to them—otherwise they'll be calling

Venture Capitalists

If you've already started up and have initial revenues, an experienced management team, and a clear plan to sell the business or go public someday, you could be ready to approach venture capitalists. These professional investors manage large funds of money—into the billions of dollars in some cases—that have been pooled from all sorts of sources, including wealthy individuals and large pension funds looking for a higher rate of return than traditional investments can provide.

During the dot-com era, raising money became synonymous with raising venture capital. Venture capitalists were uncharacteristically funding pure startups. Their strategy at that time was to start a business, throw a bunch of capital at it, grow it quickly, and then take it public and cash out through an IPO, an initial public offering. The time between startup and going public was radically condensed—from several years to less than a year in

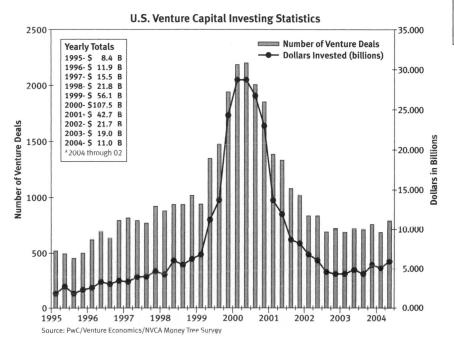

U.S. Venture Capital Investing Statistics

Yearly Totals
1995- $ 8.4 B
1996- $ 11.9 B
1997- $ 15.5 B
1998- $ 21.8 B
1999- $ 56.1 B
2000- $107.5 B
2001- $ 42.7 B
2002- $ 21.7 B
2003- $ 19.0 B
2004- $ 11.0 B
^2004 through 02

Number of Venture Deals
Dollars Invested (billions)

Source: PwC/Venture Economics/NVCA Money Tree Survey

some cases—as the public markets ravenously consumed any and all IPOs sent their way. And it worked really well for a period of time. But those stock-market-on-steroids days are over and venture capitalists have now retreated back to the safer territory of investing in later-stage companies.

Like angels, venture capitalists receive equity in exchange for their investment. However, unlike angels, venture capitalists generally require some heavy-handed measures of control over your business. And you must be prepared to focus on an "exit event"—that IPO or sale of the business that positions the holders of the equity for a return on their investment. Don't pursue venture capital if you want to grow old with your business and perhaps hand it off to your children one day. Venture capital is for fast-growth companies that have a clear plan to be grown quickly and exited.

VENTURE CAPITALISTS

Amount of Capital Available

- $1,000,000 to tens of millions

Upside ↑

- They invest smarts and networking in addition to money
- They can provide large sums of money that can be used to grow exponentially
- Once they invest in your company, they're a good source of additional capital if you need more money in the future
- They're helpful in bringing about exit opportunities for your business

Downside ↓

- They rarely invest in pure startups—and when they do it must be a fast-growth company
- They typically require you to already have experienced management and the beginnings of revenue
- You must be willing to give up a significant amount of control
- As an exit strategy, you must be interested in selling the business or doing an IPO

Equity Rules

Whether you're best suited to seek investment from angels or from venture capitalists, here are two things to keep in mind so you don't raise money just to find yourself "workin' for the man."

Do your homework. When receiving funding through an equity investment, be very sensitive as to who's providing the capital. Unlike debt financing from banks, equity funding sources are very "present." Equity investors are owners in your company. You have to report to them and you'll have to answer to them. So choose wisely—make sure you're confident that the investor is someone whose expectations are clearly aligned with yours.

Don't lose control. You'll likely have to give up some measure of control to the investor, but at the very least, make sure you retain control of the day-to-day operations of the company; remain free to operate the business as you deem appropriate. Too many times, entrepreneurs are so tantalized by the thought of raising money that they end up making a bad deal and losing control. You may end up getting the money but losing your company in the process. Don't let this happen to you.

Networking with the Money People

We often hear from radio show listeners that they have a hard time getting a meeting with money people. We know how tough this can be, given that we were once the intermediaries between entrepreneurs and our angel investors. But we have a few tips to help you meet your dream financiers.

QUICK TIP

Learn from Rejection

If you are turned down by an investor, always ask why and seek advice.

By doing so, you will learn how to modify your presentation so your odds of success increase the next time you make your pitch.

Ask the Professionals. The next time you check in with your attorney or CPA, ask if they'd be willing to introduce you to any of their clients or contacts who may be angel investors, venture capitalists, or successful entrepreneurs. An introduction like this can not only help lead to investors, but comes with credibility as well. You're more likely to get a meeting this way.

Introduce Yourself to Other Entrepreneurs Who've Raised Money. Identify businesses in your community that have successfully raised the type of capital you're seeking. Then make a point of meeting those business owners and ask them if they'd be willing to make an introduction for you. If they believe in what you're doing with your startup, they may be willing to arrange an introduction for you.

Attend Conferences and Networking Events. Serious investors often attend business conferences and networking events in order to stay in tune with emerging trends and hot opportunities. You should be there too. You never know who'll be seated at your luncheon table or getting a refill at the coffee stand at these kinds of events. Don't be shy—get out and press the flesh!

Do Some Old-fashioned Hobnobbing. We've all heard about amazing deals made on the golf course. Get out there. It's just common knowledge that people with money and time on their hands hang out at country clubs and yacht clubs, and attend charity, religious, and social events, so make sure you're there as well. You can also find them at community organizations like the Rotary or Kiwanis Club. Have business cards printed and keep them with you at all times. When you hand out a card, don't hesitate to ask the person for one of theirs—that way you can be sure you'll have the chance to make contact again. And remember our discussion about the importance of having an "elevator pitch" ready? *Be prepared to give the pitch of a lifetime!*

Check Out Your Local Angel Networks. Many communities have clubs or associations formed by angels. In Arizona, there's the Arizona Angels (www.arizonaangels.com). In New York, there's the New York Angels (www.newyorkangels.com). Portland, Oregon, has the Portland Angel Network (www.oef.com), and southern California has the Tech Coast Angels (www.techcoastangels.com). You get the idea. Many times you can get on an agenda to pitch your opportunity in front of groups like this. To find out if similar groups exist in your community, do a simple Internet search.

Prime the Pump. Don't wait until you need money to begin making connections with the money guys. Put yourself in the shoes of any big-time investor. Would you be more likely to listen to a pitch from a total stranger or someone who had built up a rapport with you? You can begin building this relationship by sending monthly e-mails to some of the investors you've met through your networking. Give them a quick report on what you're doing with your business. Highlight your successes and talk about milestones that you've met. You could make the occasional phone call or even invite them to lunch. The important point here is to work your network of contacts so when you're ready to make your pitches, you'll be well positioned.

Our Bottom Line

Just like Goldilocks, you have to find the funding that's "just right." Some will be too complicated and some too risky. Some will offer too little and some too much. But if you do your homework, consider all your options carefully, and make the "just right" contacts, you'll be on your way to getting the money you need to start up.

If you need more ideas to get you started, click on www.start-upnation.com/goldilocksapproach.

A Soaring Success

Cirrus Design Corporation

Vital Stats
- Year Founded: 1986
- 2004 Revenue: $190 million
- No. of Employees: 900
- Headquarters: Duluth, Minnesota
- For Radio Interview: www.startupnation.com/book

Big Idea
Build the safest, most consumer-friendly small airplane in the industry—complete with a parachute that can be deployed in case of an emergency.

Our next Super Startup shows how a concern for safety led to a breakthrough idea. Here's the exchange we had with Alan and Dale Klapmeier on StartupNation Radio in January 2004.

SLOAN BROTHERS: This is a company we're so excited to bring on the show. . . . Here's the thing that got us so interested in talking to you: You put parachutes on your airplanes. That's a pretty big distinction in the marketplace, isn't it?

ALAN AND DALE: That's a very big distinction! Right now we're the only company that does that on a certified manufactured general-aviation aircraft.

SLOAN BROTHERS: One of the stats we learned about your company is that 40 percent of your planes are sold to first-time buyers. So that innovation must be contributing to your growth rate, the fastest in the industry?

ALAN AND DALE: That, and we've added other features to make it truly comfortable and easy to fly—to make it appealing to the "traveler" more than just the "aviation enthusiast."

As you listen to the rest of the interview, you hear in the Klapmeiers' voices a level of passion that is pure and extreme for what they do. Here's why. Years earlier, in 1985, Alan Klapmeier was almost finished with a flying lesson when the worst happened. Two miles out from the airstrip at Sauk Prairie Airport in Wisconsin, his plane collided with another at 1,600 feet. The two planes began plummeting to earth. Alan and his instructor began the frantic, complex measures to bring their plane under control. They barely managed to land the plane safely. The other aircraft slammed into the ground. Its pilot did not survive.

Instead of grounding Alan for life, walking away from the accident made him even more determined to turn a childhood dream into a real business. He and his brother envisioned building small commercial airplanes with safety features that would make them competitive against the industry leader, Cessna. As crazy as it sounded, their planes would have a unique feature: a parachute that would float the entire plane to earth in the case of an emergency. Armed with their own know-how and this revolutionary idea, the two brothers cleared out their parents' barn in Baraboo, Wisconsin, and began work on their first airplane.

Over the next two decades, the brothers faced huge obstacles—including the deaths of two test pilots and an engine fire that almost put them out of business. But in the end, the Klapmeiers prevailed. They succeeded in turning their dream into Cirrus Design— a major force in the private aviation industry, with the first-ever "plane parachute," which has already saved six lives since Cirrus delivered its first airplanes in 1999. What's more, in just three short years their planes have become the top seller in the industry, dethroning Cessna, which had held that position for decades. No airplanes in the history of general aviation have enjoyed such instant popularity as those made by Cirrus Design.

The Klapmeiers' story is truly inspiring for any business owner. Not only did their idea for a business save lives, but Dale and Alan's story illustrates perfectly how two people with passion and a dream can succeed against all odds.

They started their odyssey without a lot of money or manufacturing expertise. Initially, the Klapmeiers decided to try their hand with kits for build-your-own airplanes. They wanted to avoid the costly and time-consuming commercial approvals that the Federal Aviation Administration places on manufactured airplanes. The kit planes were appealing to quirky flying enthusiasts like themselves. For the Klapmeiers, just two kids out of college (as Dale describes the two of them), kits were a quick and easy way to get into the business of selling planes.

By 1987, the two brothers were ready to unveil their first kit airplane at the famous Oshkosh Air Show, where hundreds of thousands of flying enthusiasts congregate each year to see the latest and greatest innovations in planes.

"We thought we'd be overwhelmed. We even talked about who would take orders and who would direct traffic," Dale recounts. The reality: Hardly anyone stopped by to see their plane and they didn't get a single order. While the two brothers had built a plane that they loved, the complex, hard-to-fly, hard-to-build plane didn't really offer anything new to the industry. It was an eye-opening moment for the brothers, one they would carry with them throughout the next 20 years in business. They realized that they'd not only failed their target audience, they'd failed themselves and their dream. The plane simply wasn't the safe, easy-to-fly airplane that Alan had envisioned after his midair collision.

Smarting from the failure, the two brothers went back to the drawing board in their barn. They were determined this time to really work on their dream of building a comfortable, easy-to-fly, safe airplane. And to make sure they'd design a plane that was appealing to the market, they began to listen to consumers.

According to Dale, "When you talk to pilots, they want a fast, cool plane with a macho image. But talk to people at the malls in Madison and you get a different picture. If they've been up in a small airplane, they'll tell you how much fun it can be looking down from the skies. But then ask them if they've ever thought of becoming a pilot, and the answer is always 'No.' They worry about how hard it must be to learn to fly. The planes are loud, uncomfortable, and seem unsafe."

With all of this consumer feedback fresh in their minds, Dale and Alan built an all-new kit airplane. "We removed all the dials and gadgets and replaced them with computer screens that were easy to read. We put in windows that were large enough to really see out of. We made it comfortable to sit in," he says.

Shortly before the 1989 Oshkosh Air Show, Alan took the new plane up for a test run. A few minutes into the flight, smoke started billowing out of the engine. The plane had caught fire in midair. For the second time in five years, Alan was forced to make an emergency landing. Safely on the ground, all Alan could do was watch as the fire spread and the plane and the brothers' hopes went up in smoke.

Once again they went back to the barn with a new plan, a plan to finally build the commercially viable, FAA-certified plane that had been on their minds since Alan's midair collision in 1985.

They began work on a prototype that would include the creature comforts they had gleaned from their kit plane research. But most important, the plane would finally be outfitted with the safety feature the brothers felt could change general aviation forever: a parachute that attached to the top of the plane and could be deployed in an emergency.

"We went back to one of the original insights from regular everyday consumers: They were afraid for their lives when they were in a small airplane," Dale said. "With our parachute, even if something really bad happens, it doesn't mean everybody has to die."

It would take another nine years of diligence to move from that important insight to a manufacturing plant that now produces more than 550 airplanes a year. They funded the project through various means, including 240 individual investors whose money helped them build prototypes and test the parachutes. The investments ranged from a few thousand dollars to a few million dollars. In 2001, a venture capital firm, Crescent Capital, made a $100 million investment that enabled the company to transition from producing a limited number of planes to turning out more than 500 each year.

In an attempt to become experts in FAA certification, the Klapmeiers asked every question they could think of. "We had engineers read through every regulation. From 1992 to 1993, we lived and breathed certification," Dale says. Such attention to detail paid off when it came time to certify. The Klapmeiers even told the FAA they wanted the certification rules changed so that they didn't have to prove they could pull their plane out of a self-induced spin before it crashed. "It's a quirk of the industry that certification requires you to put a plane into spin. We had created a plane that wouldn't go into a spin." Their team was so well versed in the regulations that the FAA acquiesced. Dale and Alan were on their way to seeing their dream finally become a reality—fully 10 years after Alan's first midair emergency.

But in 1998, disaster struck yet again, and this time the consequences were tragic. Their prototype plane was ready for a flight test. It had all the innovative features that the Klapmeiers' planes would become known for—except one. It was not yet equipped with their parachute, which was still a few weeks away from being ready. During the test flight, something malfunctioned in the plane and the test pilot, Scott Anderson, could not bring it under control. Much to the horror of everyone involved, the plane crashed and took Scott's life.

Going on after Scott's death, Dale tells us, was the toughest thing the two brothers had ever done. "But we had to move on, we had to keep going, because we didn't want there to be any more tragedies like Scott's."

A year later, in 1999, Cirrus Designs delivered its first airplane, complete with the plane parachute that would have saved Scott's life. To this day, Dale says he keeps a picture of Scott hanging in his office. "I look at him every day. He's what makes this business so meaningful to us."

The Klapmeiers' Key Moves

1. **Passion and Commitment.** The Klapmeiers never stopped believing in themselves and the merit of their innovations. They had the will to follow through on their dream no matter what stood in their way. Alan and Dale proved that nearly any obstacle can be overcome with the right doses of passion and commitment.

2. **Listening to Customers.** Sometimes entrepreneurs can be their own worst enemy. They design their offering based on their own assumptions without really investigating what the mar-

ket wants. After failing initially, the Klapmeiers turned to potential customers to better understand what their needs were and how to address them. Their industry-leading sales record illustrates how important it is to listen to customers.

3. **Expertise.** The Klapmeiers became "thought leaders" in their field. By immersing themselves in the requirements of the FAA and learning everything there was to know about their industry, the brothers could affect the environment in which they were doing business. They were able to engineer a breakthrough product and influence the FAA to rewrite rules that had been in existence for decades. As the Klapmeiers demonstrate, expertise is a pivotal asset for entrepreneurs. It allows you to think in innovative ways, make great products, understand the market, make informed decisions, and, just as Alan and Dale have done, plot a course for a soaring success.

4. **Goldilocks Approach.** The Klapmeiers are poster children for finding the right money at the right time. They first lined up angel investors for small amounts of money. Then they proceeded to involve much larger angel investments as their company grew. Ultimately, they stepped up to a major venture capital investment of $100 million that launched their business into the stratosphere.

CHAPTER SEVEN

The Power of People

"Sloan Brothers, Tear Down That Wall!"

In November 2000, we decided it was time to move our business out of the basement of Jeff's house, where we'd worked for eight years. We had our eye on a building in Birmingham's bustling downtown for a long time. The three-story structure was on the north end of Old Woodward, our town's "Main Street." The building was within walking distance of our homes and our favorite restaurants and across the street from a small park. What we loved best about the second-story space was the big front office with huge windows that filled the rooms with natural light all day long. After almost a decade of working out of the windowless basement at home, we were finally going to see the sunlight and the change of seasons!

But as soon as we signed the lease, we ran into a sticky situation: how to divide up the front office between the two of us. For the first few years in the basement, we'd used the same desk and the same computer to save money. We sat on opposite sides of the desk, and when one of us wanted to use the computer or comment on the other's work, we'd simply swivel the computer around. This was obviously not a sustainable solution—we squabbled incessantly (and then laughed about our spats at the end of each day)—so we eventually separated ourselves by kicking in for separate, updated computers with separate desks, about 10 feet apart. That actually worked well for several years.

Still, the thought of moving into a "real," window-wrapped, fancy office was absolutely thrilling. Not only did we have a space that served our needs, but now we would be able to hire a number of partners and employees who'd been working with us part-time.

Upon signing the lease, we built handsome individual offices for each of them. We put in two big desks for us at opposite ends of the front office. Our desks, as the *Wall Street Journal* reported in a 2003 feature article, were now 18 feet apart (the reporter actually measured with a tape measure). We filled the space between the desks with a large, comfortable black leather couch, two chairs, and a coffee table so that our growing staff could hang out and carry on meetings with both of us in a casual environment.

Sharing an office had always been one of the keys to our success. Instead of having to traipse down the hallway, or worse, pick up the phone to talk to each other about a great idea, a crucial investment, or a new business plan we'd received, we could discuss it immediately. Such close communication meant that we made decisions quickly and were able to resolve issues before they became problems. We perfected the art of lip reading, eye contact, and hand signals.

We loved our new open office. Our staff members, who inhabited the other 3,000 square feet of the office, loved it as well because they could talk to both of us at the same time. And our investors and the executives in our portfolio companies immediately warmed to the idea of a place where they could sit and chat with us instead of having to book a conference room, as they did with other more conventional companies.

Our shared office arrangement wasn't that unusual, however. Michael Dell and his chief executive officer, Kevin Rollins, share a 40-foot office with a sliding glass partition that they say has never been closed. Even big traditional companies have adopted the practice. A. G. Lafley, the CEO of Procter & Gamble, shares an open office space with the head of human resources, Richard Antoine, and vice chairman, Bruce Byrnes.

The open office was working great until the spring of 2004, when StartupNation really started experiencing explosive growth. We were busier than ever, preparing for our weekly radio show, conducting online seminars, coaching entrepreneurs, and making sure our corporate sponsors were satisfied. We were writing newsletters and columns for our growing community at Startup-Nation.com. Rich was still sitting on the boards of our portfolio companies, such as Rubicon Genomics and Clarity Technologies, which were finally back on track and gaining ground after the recession of 2001–2002. Jeff was hatching a new idea for a company called SmartCollector that we were preparing to launch at eBay Live! in June 2004.

On any given day, the office became the location for a board meeting, an investment presentation, a brainstorming session, or a branding consultation. Some days, it felt like all of those activities were swirling around us all at once. Our growing staff, accustomed to popping into our office and having instant access to both of us at the same time, frequently interrupted us and distracted us from the work that absolutely, positively had to be done that day.

The activity in our shared office, once so *important* to getting business done, was starting to *stand in the way* of getting anything done. Instead of helping us, it seemed to be hindering us, breaking our concentration and interrupting our calls. We didn't want to throw out our open-door policy.

One night we started talking about what we could do to make

life easier and get us back on track. One possible remedy after another got rejected, until we were left with a final solution: It was time to grow up a little, act like real bosses with offices that had doors and walls.

Without notifying anyone on the team, we called our contractor and told him to construct a solid wall down the middle of our open office. A massive oak door was ordered to go between our two offices. Over a weekend, the wall went up. On Monday, as each of our employees walked in, the looks on their faces reflected their shock. They were crestfallen. Out in the hallway, they started whispering, "What's wrong with Jeff and Rich?" Then, on Tuesday, just as the odor of the fresh paint had started to fade, our employees—never shrinking violets—began complaining. The most popular phrase by the end of that day was a good-natured joke that paid homage to Ronald Reagan during the Cold War.

"Sloan Brothers, tear down this wall!" the employees all yelled at us as they left the offices that night.

But there was something very serious behind their joke. We hadn't realized that our open office had done more than keep communication going between the two of us. Our shared space had come to stand as a symbol for something bigger at StartupNation. It was a symbol of how inclusive our business was, how important employee participation was, and how critical communication was between everyone in the business, not just between us. By putting up the wall, we'd done more than separate ourselves. We'd put up a wall between our staff and ourselves. In erecting that wall, we'd stripped StartupNation of what had made it such a unique place to work.

Three weeks later, while in New Orleans at the eBay Live! Conference, we secretly called the carpenters and told them, "Go into the office this weekend and *tear down that wall!*"

The "wall incident," as it's become known around the office, illustrates many of the reasons why we believe people are the key component to making a business flourish. It was a huge mistake not to include input from the staff members in the decision. Only after tearing down the wall did we realize that the shared space and the open-door policy meant more to them than we had ever imagined.

Since the wall came down, StartupNation has been a better place to work. The wall underscored another element about our business that we had apparently begun to take for granted: the idea that the soul of our business, and a big part of what made us love it, was the people factor. It was our interaction with one another and the rest of the team that made the work about so much more than a financial bottom line.

Finding Your Superstars

We were lucky. We each found our best business partner sitting across the kitchen table when we were just two young boys growing up in Flint.

Over the years, however, we've devised a strategy to bring more "brothers" and "sisters" into our business by keeping a running log of the people we meet. The list is made up of people we've met in our personal and professional lives. They're people we felt immediately connected to, who shared our enthusiasm for great ideas and bold new ventures. Some of them have great skills that we think we might need in our businesses at some future date. Some simply show great potential or great passion for the entrepreneurial life. Others are power brokers who may never work *for* us but will work *with* us to help us achieve our goals.

We never had a formal name for our list of people until Joel Welsh, our chief community officer, came to work for us in 2004. When we sat down to talk to him on his first day on the job, he told us about his superstar list: a list of people whom he wanted to either work for, work with, or simply get to know at some point in his life. We were on the list. He always kept 12 people on the list and rarely let it dip below 10. He even had a strategy for checking in once a month with at least one person on the list.

Joel's system mirrored our own beliefs about how you find great people to work with—whether they become employees, partners, or mentors. You look for three types of people when you're filling up your superstar list: people with potential, people with proven skills, and people who are what we call "power brokers."

Power Brokers. They not only have great skills that you need but they also wield influence in your community or industry. Power brokers—by the nature of who they are, what they've accomplished, and the respect they command—can help you with advice, contacts, credibility, and other invaluable contributions. We've had the good fortune to have many power brokers come in and out of our lives. Here are some examples of power brokers to show you the kinds of qualities they have and what they can bring to your business.

One of the first was our attorney, Ira Jaffe, managing partner of Jaffe, Raitt, Heuer & Weiss, P.C. Ira is a power broker in Detroit. When we were getting our start in trying to commercialize the Battery Buddy, Ira took us under his wing. He not only lent his legal and business expertise to our project, but he also lent us an air of credibility because he was so highly esteemed in our business community.

John Auman, whom we introduced earlier in discussing the development of the Battery Buddy, was a power broker with contacts in the automotive engineering field. Engineers he recruited came onboard readily just because they would jump at a chance to work with John.

Frank Hennessey of Hennessey Capital is yet another power broker. In addition to having been CEO of several public corporations, Frank was the chairman of the Detroit Regional Chamber of Commerce, the biggest chamber in the country. Frank became intrigued with what we were doing at Sloan Ventures and wanted to learn about investment opportunities. He found a trove of fascinating businesses in our portfolio and a real resonance with our team. Frank not only ended up providing personal monetary investment, he brought a group of motivated and capable high-net-worth angel investors as well. Since then, Frank has become a mentor, always advising us on business strategies and opportunities.

People with Proven Skills. Reserve several positions on your superstar list for people with proven skills. These are the people who'll fill in where you're weak. They round out your team and prove the adage that the sum is greater than the parts.

We're always on the lookout for people with proven skills. No matter where we go, we watch how people work, what they love to do, and what they do well. You can find these people anywhere, but a good place to connect is during conferences or when you work on a big project with a lot of other people. Sometimes an event can be a gold mine for a superstar list, and that was definitely true of Digital Detroit. The annual conference pulled together droves of enthusiastic, passionate people—some anonymous, some luminaries—who wanted to build business and technology opportunities. Through Digital Detroit, we met several people whom we put on our list, including Stephanie Jacobson, our prized communications director and now a partner in our holding company. These kinds of events are abundant all around the country, and we urge you to seek them out, shake hands,

QUICK TIP

Hire for Personality

Your superstars have to make up your team. And it's the team that will create or derail your success. So personalities are often just as important as skills.

shoot the breeze, and discover the people who are out there that may just be your superstars.

People with Potential. We'll admit it can be a little scary hiring people for potential as opposed to hiring for proven skills. But it's a strategy that's worked well for us. Hiring for potential is exactly what we did to position Clarity Technologies for success.

In 1997, we met Gail Erten, PhD, the young, bright scientist from Cal Tech, whom we discussed earlier in the book. She was working on software that enabled microphones to filter out undesirable background sounds. She'd started her research for the Department of Defense, but after we'd talked to her briefly, the many commercial applications for her work became obvious—things like computers, cars, and cell phones.

At the time, she was looking for outside investors to help see her through her research. We knew she and her work had a great deal of potential, and we decided to embark on the creation of a company and viable business plan that would be attractive to angel investors. We launched Clarity Technologies, Inc., weeks later.

It was the start of a great working relationship with Gail. The project, however, was missing a chief executive who could take what was basically a scientific research project and turn it into a real business. We'd come across several candidates through our network of "superstars," and we introduced Gail to one of them. A former Sony executive, he had years of experience in the sound and audio business. We thought he would make for a great fit with the technology because of its audio applications. But after just a few months of working with him, it became obvious to all of us that we'd picked wrong. He was very versed in audio technology and the ways of big corporations, but he wasn't in his element running a small startup company. By late 1998, Clarity and this executive parted ways.

We sat down with Gail to determine just what had gone wrong.

What we needed was someone who could shepherd the business through the grueling years of finding investors, keeping the technology on track, and hiring great people who could help make Clarity into a successful business.

We started sifting through names. One that Rich kept coming back to was Ray Gunn; he'd met Ray through a referral, and quickly added him to his superstar list. Ray had been a second-in-command for years at several startups in the medical device market, and he was champing at the bit to run a company himself. While he had never hung the "CEO" sign on his office door, we believed this guy had great potential.

Rich

He had that "take that hill" kind of mentality that you need to really push a startup forward. Plus he had charisma and communication skills, and deep experience in raising money and scoping out new markets for technology. He was a risk-taker, a leader, but he was also a doer. And that's exactly what we needed to help fill the weaknesses in the company.

With Ray at the helm, the company took off. Under his leadership, Clarity has won numerous industry awards for innovation and technology. In his first effort as CEO, Ray has raised over $10 million in funding from sophisticated investors and run a high-tech startup like a well-oiled machine. He's amassed a dream list of customers and built a loyal and inspired staff beneath him. He's proof positive that hiring for potential can work—and work well. Ray has flourished in the role, so much so that we now call on him when we're looking for some perspective on how to deal with certain leadership challenges or business opportunities. We consider him to be one of the quintessential startup leaders we know.

Ray's Three People Pointers

Ray knows who to hire. However, Ray has also learned who *not* to hire. Although Ray is proud, and rightly so, of low turnover rates among his employees, he has had to fire three senior executives he once thought were perfect for his team. Here is what he learned from these experiences:

1. **Don't try to fit round pegs into square holes.** Ray hired a respected engineer from Lucent at one point. "She had all the right credentials and she came from a large, established company I respected. She was a huge win for us. But it ended up being a terrible cultural fit. She didn't understand that we didn't have 'process' for everything. We just needed to get things done and then we'd think about how we got there. As a startup, we needed people who could go with that kind of chaotic flow. She couldn't get comfortable with the idea that sometimes you're pretty sloppy when you first start out and in a small business life is pretty unstructured. I pulled her aside one day and simply said, 'You're not happy here, and we should find a place where you will be happy.'" Ray made a mistake that's easy to make—one we've seen other companies make. You hire people who look great on paper but simply aren't a good fit within a startup culture. Be sure *your* hires blend with your existing team, both personally as well as professionally.

2. **Don't promise what you can't deliver.** At one point, Ray was trying to expand Clarity's presence on the West Coast. "I found this guy who was passionate about coming on board, but I couldn't meet his salary. I told him that we were early stage and we could give him 80 percent of what he wanted. We brought him on, but for the next six months he focused more on renegotiating the pay package than building our business. I called him into my office and said, 'I can't afford you, and I should have recognized it before I hired you. We didn't listen to each other's expectations.'" Keeping your salaries under control is critically important, especially in the early stages of a startup. While you should always aim to hire the best and brightest for the job, don't let them hold you hostage to a pay package you can't afford yet.

3. **New blood that turns into bad blood.** Adding new blood to a company is a great way to raise the bar with your existing employees. But do it the wrong way and you end up having bad blood throughout the company. As Clarity expanded, Ray decided to hire a new vice president of sales whom many people ended up resenting. "I wanted to hire this person to run our wireless sales for a year before I promoted him to vice-president status. But he was desperate for the title. So I asked one of my best people to move aside to make room. It was a huge failure. He had enemies in the company before he even started—from the people he was overseeing to the person I'd asked to move aside. He couldn't do anything without someone undermining him." It's a common mistake. You want to add new skills to your company, especially if you're trying to buttress existing weaknesses. But you have to be careful of the rest of the group's feelings toward the new hire. If you really believe you need a new person on the team, take the time to get the buy-in from your other employees.

Keeping Your Stars

Once you've hired your superstars, be sure to do more than just pay their salaries and benefits, as there's a lot of competition for desirable employees. Offer benefits that will keep your employees happy and make them less likely to jump ship. One of the telltale signs of a strong company is its employee-retention rate. The longer your employees stay around and remain happy, the more successful your company is going to be.

Here are some ways to retain your staff.

Customized perks. Determine what perks are important to your employees. Many perks, such as the turkey at Thanksgiving or the predictable Christmas bonus, are a holdover from more traditional times. Even stock options—the carrot used too often in the dot-com days—may not be a huge motivation for employees if it will take years for them to cash out. Instead of assuming you know what they want, ask them. You may find that instead of a monthly parking pass, your chief financial officer would rather have a gym membership. Get creative! Your engineers may want a more flexible work schedule instead of the regular two weeks' vacation. Customization is a great way to compete against bigger companies who can offer your employees bigger salaries and better benefits. Big companies can't easily customize benefits to staffs of hundreds or thousands. But as a small business, you have that kind of flexibility. *Use it*. Remember—the perks don't have to have huge monetary value. Focus instead on what makes the perk important to that specific employee.

Recognize the whole team. It may seem counterintuitive to take a team approach when we're talking about retaining employees. But the workplace is like any other community. Just as people like to be part of a thriving neighborhood or city, people like to be a part of a thriving, successful team at work. While some people thrive on being the "MIP," the most important person in a company, most of us really like working on teams where we all get equal representation and equal recognition. In fact, building up superstar status for a few people can be destructive to your small business. If you want to give credit, give credit to an entire team by taking them all out for lunch. Jack Aronson builds teamwork and recognizes everyone with the monthly barbecue he holds at Garden Fresh Gourmet. Jack cooks for his entire staff—about 80 people—and gives the whole company—from the factory crews that come in at 5 A.M. to the front-office staff—a chance to catch up with each other, to talk about new babies, weddings, and family news.

Communicate more than you think you need to. Too often, small-business owners make the mistake of believing that communication will just happen in a company. They think that employees will know what's going on in the minds of management or in the daily running of the business. While it might seem like overkill to hold update meetings—whether that includes you and your partner or the five people in your office—it's important to share key information at least once a week. By getting that regular face time, you can anticipate challenges that are about to bubble up and conquer existing ones before they derail your company. The meetings don't have to be long. Even a five-minute chat around your desk on a Monday morning can make all the difference.

On Your Own? Get a Mentor

If you work alone at home, you know just how lonely it can get. While there's a lot of flexibility (and the commute is a breeze), your business can stagnate if you don't get exposure to new ideas. That's why we suggest to business owners, especially those who intend to—or already do—work alone, to recruit a mentor to give them advice, offer moral support, and break up the routine. A mentor is someone who can offer you wisdom, creativity, connections, accountability, credibility, and fresh thinking about your business.

Do you need help with marketing or operations? Could you tweak your service to win a whole new set of customers? Do you need contacts in a specific community? Once you've answered a few questions like those, start working your Rolodex.

Once you've struck up a relationship, consider making your interactions structured. Meet at least once a quarter to discuss your business. Note: It's critical to make sure that your mentor is willing to challenge you. Encouragement and loyalty are important, but don't let them get in the way of honest and blunt dialogue.

QUICK TIP

Manage Your Meetings

Our events director at StartupNation is Jessica Schlick—the most organized person we know! Here are her thoughts on how to make the most of meetings with team members, customers, and vendors:

"Some meetings involve reporting and analysis. Some are creative sessions focused on innovation. In either case, make sure you circulate an agenda in advance so everyone can prepare. Set clear objectives in the agenda. Include the amount of time you plan to spend on each agenda item and assign responsibility where appropriate. If your meeting strays from the agenda, don't be rigid—you wouldn't want to squelch out a productive discussion. Just make sure you continuously monitor the clock so you cover everything you need to."

If you plan to grow your business beyond just yourself and your home office, you may want to expand your mentor strategy. You might want to step up from a single individual to building a multimember advisory board.

Just remember—whether it involves a mentor or a full advisory board—be sure you keep them informed. As the adage goes, "out of sight, out of mind." To really get value out of your mentors, you've got to figure out ways to keep your business in their mental crosshairs.

Customers Are People, Too

You've taken care of your employees by rewarding them. You've taken care of yourself by setting up a board of advisors. Who's left in the people equation of your business? Your customer.

Never, ever forget your customers. You simply cannot survive without them. They pay the bills, they ultimately pay your salary, and their dollars and cents help grow your business day after day. It seems so simple to say and so obvious. But all too often, priorities wander and customers go starved for attention. It's hard to imagine why this would happen given how important customers are to a company's success. Quite literally, your business would be nowhere without the people who buy your products. So treating those people extremely well should be the No. 1 goal of every company. But we all know that's often not the case. We've all been customers and consumers who at one time or another have been treated poorly by surly counter staff, obnoxious call-center employees, rude salespeople, and so on and so on.

It doesn't have to be that way, and it shouldn't be that way in your business if you expect to do more than survive. By offering great customer service, no matter what you sell, make, or deliver, you'll be way ahead of the competition. Give great customer service, and people will keep coming back. They'll tell their friends about you, and you'll get the benefit of word-of-mouth marketing, the best kind of marketing there is and something no amount of money can buy.

But creating a business that gives great customer service isn't easy—especially as your small business grows. While you may be great at serving your customers, how do you teach new employees to treat customers the way you do? How do you make customer service a top priority when there's so much work to do just to keep the business up and running? Those same questions have bedeviled thousands of companies. But there are some companies that stand head and shoulders above everyone else when it comes to great customer service. One of them is a favorite business of ours: a deli turned specialty food juggernaut called Zingerman's. The deli was started by Ari Weinzweig and Paul Saginaw more than 20 years ago in an old brick building in Ann Arbor, Michigan. Their phenomenal success has turned them into a statewide tradition and a consulting service for food and hospitality businesses across the country. It's got such panache that it was featured on the cover of *Inc.* in 2003 and was named "The Coolest Small Company in America."

On any day of the week, starting at around 11 A.M. and lasting until about 2 P.M., the line for a Zingerman's sandwich queues up and snakes past the deli counter, filled with cheeses and meats, and goes right out the front door. Having a line of waiting customers sounds like a recipe for disaster in customer service: a long line of really hungry people with a short lunch hour. But rarely do you hear people complain; more often you hear how terrific the service is at Zingerman's; what sandwich someone tried and loved last week; why they wouldn't think of eating lunch anywhere else.

QUICK TIP

QUICK TIP

While it's common to focus heavily on bringing new customers in to grow profits and revenues, don't forget that existing customers can be even more important to your bottom line. It takes valuable time and marketing dollars to bring in new customers—up to five times more than it does to keep an existing customer. And it takes even more time and money to bring a disgruntled customer back. So it really does save you money to find ways to keep your existing customers happy.

We finally decided to learn firsthand how Zingerman's creates such superior customer service. So we invited Ari to come on StartupNation Radio to talk about his approach. Zingerman's is built on the basic theory that by offering great customer service, one customer at a time, the company will thrive. They started with just two employees and $500,000 in sales in 1983, and grew to 259 employees and $14 million in sales in 2003. The company has expanded beyond the deli to include online sales, a bakery, and a restaurant.

We asked Ari for his tips on customer service. The first thing he did was give us a small paperback book he self-published in 2003 called *Zingerman's Guide to Giving Great Service: Treating Our Customers Like Royalty*. Now, you know a company is serious about customer service, not just sandwiches, when it distills its customer-service philosophy into a 130-page bible. The now dog-eared book has become one of our favorite reads, with its practical advice on how to make customer service a priority across the board for employees and owners. While we can't give you all of the nuggets of wisdom you'll find in the book, here are some of our favorite tips (reprinted with kind permission from Ari and Hyperion, which published the book for a national audience in late 2004) on how to create the best customer service possible, no matter what business you're in.

ARI'S CUSTOMER SERVICE TIPS

- **Write down the mission statement of your company and include a customer-service component.** While Ari is quick to point out that oftentimes mission statements are meaningless, if written properly they can be used just like the North Star to navigate by. "No matter how lost or frustrated we may feel on any given day, it's always there, much like the North Star, to help give us a general sense of direction."
- **Make it real.** To make the mission statement more than something you print on a plaque, you have to put guts behind it. Put in place

systems that help, instead of hinder, customer service. As Ari says he tells his staff, "You can't eat good intentions for dinner." Once you've made it your mission to provide good service, give employees the tools to make it happen. Ari has instituted a four-check system to make certain orders are taken accurately—so you don't get corned beef when you want pastrami on your sandwich at the deli, or cherry chocolate bread when you wanted sourdough in your online order. Instill in your employees the bottom-line value of giving good customer service—and not just that it brings in more money. One of our favorites from Ari is the concept that giving good customer service means easier work over the long haul. "It almost always ends up being easier to do things well and make the customer's experience something special than do a slipshod job and have to clean up the mess later," according to Ari.

- **Respect customer service.** Ari points out, rightly so, that giving service just isn't something we're taught to do in America; serving is sort of a low rung on the ladder of what we want to be known for here. Instead, he says, we need to see serving as an "honorable profession." While Ari is talking specifically about the service profession—waiting tables, making deli sandwiches, and ringing up purchases—we think service is a part of any business. Respecting the importance of serving others—whether it be your suppliers, your coworker, or the mother buying your baby food online—is key to giving great service.

- And finally, perhaps the most important tip we've taken from Ari and the Zingerman's manual on customer service is this: **Define what you mean by customer service and then measure the results.** Spell out in clear, definitive terms what you mean by customer service. It's one thing to say, "The customer is always right" or "The customer is king," but what does that really mean? At Zingerman's, Ari has outlined three steps to great customer service:

1. Figure out what the customers want.

2. Get it for them accurately, politely, and enthusiastically.

3. Go the extra mile for the customer.

(continued on next page)

By defining exactly what you mean when you refer to excellent customer service in your own company, you have a better shot at providing it. After you've defined good customer service, measure the results to see if it's working and reward the people who give great service. Ari measures everything from the number of Code Reds (customer complaints) that come in every day, to repeat orders, repeat customers, and customer referrals. Ari says that watching service performance scores—measured by whatever metrics you decide are most important—can predict if you're going to have problems in the future. "When service scores start to fall off, I know that sales are likely to follow the same downward trend."

(For more information on Zingerman's customer service ideas, check out www.zingtrain.com.)

Our Bottom Line

Building Your Team. Mediocre people typically cannot make even the greatest idea into a success, whereas great people can make even a mediocre idea succeed. If you want to grow your business, hiring great people will have the greatest impact. Just make sure they complement your abilities, fit the culture, and share common values and goals.

Customer Focus. Once you've hired your stars, the next thing to focus on is superior customer service. It's easy to do, it's more pleasant dealing with happy, satisfied people, it plays to your competitive advantage as you compete with big businesses, and it increases revenue through repeat business and free word-of-mouth promotion.

Find a Niche and Fill It

Garden Fresh Gourmet, Inc.

Vital Stats

- Year Founded: 1997
- 2004 Revenue: $12 million (estimated)
- No. of Employees: 80 (including founder Jack Aronson, his daughter, and several nephews and nieces)
- Headquarters: Ferndale, Michigan
- For Radio Interview: www.startupnation.com/book

Big Idea

Create a fresh salsa with no preservatives that tastes so good it flies off the grocery shelves.

Jack Aronson's story is one that many entrepreneurs dream of. As a guest on our radio show, Jack floored us with his answer to one of our first questions:

SLOAN BROTHERS: Jack, it's an ambitious product to bring to market—it's a really crowded field! I'm curious—what's the company doing in terms of sales?

JACK: Well, we started just selling it in our restaurant; after a while, I had to move to a bigger facility. I was doing 20 pints out of the restaurant.

SLOAN BROTHERS: How many pints are you doing now?

JACK: Ummm, three million pints this year.

SLOAN BROTHERS: Wow! What are your projections going forward?

JACK: Well, we've doubled every year for the last four years. . . .

We were amazed at his rapid rise to millions in revenue. He had done what so many people wish to—taking that great recipe, packaging it up, and blowing it out the door in a big way.

Indeed, small food businesses are "a dime a dozen." But, to become successful businesses, good food ideas require that you "find a niche and fill it," as we often tell people who call in with food or restaurant ideas. Jack's ability to fill the niche of fresh salsa is the quintessential example of how to do food right.

Food is a big area of exploration for entrepreneurs-in-waiting. It's not hard to see why. Most of us love to eat and a lot of us love to cook. In fact, we bet a lot of you have thought about creating a nice little business selling cookies from your grandma's recipe book or opening a restaurant based on your favorite dishes. But there's nothing tougher than the food business. According to the SBA and other organizations, restaurants and food retailers have some of the highest failure rates of all small businesses.

And that's why "getting real" and "staying real" about your favorite food idea is so crucial. Jack Aronson and his salsa story provide a number of critical lessons for anyone interested in whipping up their favorite recipe and turning it into the next food fad. Jack was turned off by processed foods for life after a stint working in a hospital cafeteria. Over the years, he worked in and owned several restaurants, finally ending up buying a down-and-out restaurant in Ferndale, a quaint little Detroit suburb. He renamed the restaurant the Clubhouse BBQ. Always focused on fresh, quality ingredients, Jack ground his own hamburger and made his salad dressings from scratch. He started selling all kinds of homemade bottled hot sauces and barbecue sauces from the restaurant. As the trend of hotter and spicier foods took off, he was selling so much hot sauce, he opened a second location in Royal Oak, a suburb just north of Ferndale.

The Hot Zone, as Jack and his brother named it, specialized in the weirdest and wackiest hot sauces that Jack could find. It was on one of his scouting trips to New Mexico that he came up with the idea for fresh salsa.

"It was 1998 and I was down at the Fiery Food Show in Albuquerque, New Mexico. I fell in love with all the fresh salsas. All I'd ever had were those bottled salsas that have all the flavors cooked out of them. I decided then and there I wanted to make a fresh salsa for the restaurant."

That idea struck Jack like great ideas strike so many people. But *ah-hah!* moments like Jack's are more than just coincidences, and more than just luck. The fact is, Jack had his radar up. He was out "in the mix." He was in the right place at the right time to position himself for a breakthrough. It reminds us of our Gefilte Fish Philosophy.

MOLSON AND THE GEFILTE FISH PHILOSOPHY

Molson, one of the many golden retrievers we've owned over the years, had this uncanny knack for being "lucky." He always seemed to get the biggest bones or to be brought inside when the other dogs were still banished to the backyard.

(continued on next page)

But we didn't realize just what this "luck" was all about until we saw him in action during a holiday dinner back in the mid-1990s.

It was Passover and we were all gathered in the kitchen helping prepare dinner. We were ladling out the ceremonial gefilte fish, the fish equivalent of meatballs. We noticed that Molson had settled down for what looked like a nap right at our feet.

But as he rested his head on his paws, his eyes were wide open, staring up at us—alert as always. Just then, one of the pieces of fish slipped off the spoon and fell. But instead of landing on the floor, it fell directly into the open mouth of "lucky" Molson, who had instantaneously raised his head in anticipation. He didn't chew. There wasn't a sound. It just went right down his open throat.

Molson quickly licked his chops, laid his head back down on his paws, stared upward, and waited for the next piece of fish to fall.

Our lesson from Molson? You dramatically increase your odds of being "lucky" by putting yourself in the right place at the right time.

Thus was born the "Gefilte Fish Philosophy," wisdom memorialized forevermore by the smart thinking and quick acting of our golden retriever. We share this odd-named philosophy and the story behind it whenever we're trying to show that "luck" is really about the moment when opportunity meets preparation. If you want to have your own *ah-hah!* moment like Jack Aronson did, put yourself where the great ideas will fall out of the sky and hit you on the head.

Jack started experimenting with salsas. His original recipe was a little out of the ordinary—spicy artichoke-garlic salsa—handmade by Jack himself using a baby blender on a rickety card table in his kitchen. It was so spicy he decided it would be smart to taste-test the salsa at the Hot Zone store to see how customers reacted. Depending upon their feedback, he could tweak the heat level up or down.

Putting the salsa in the Hot Zone paid off. Jack learned that the customers loved his recipe. People kept coming back for more. Moreover, "Jack's Special," as he ended up naming it, caught the attention of a particularly curious customer. "One day, an owner

of a small grocery chain came up to me and said, 'I've been looking for a really good fresh salsa for 20 years, and this is the best-
tasting salsa I've ever had. Do you want to sell it in my store?'"

Jack was having another *ah-hah!* moment. Until the grocery
store owner came into the Hot Zone, Jack said he hadn't really
considered commercializing his salsas. Jack was a restaurant
owner, not a salsa maker. "You know, it was a really lunatic
idea," he says of the moment when he decided to shut down the
restaurant's dining room and start making salsa on the four stove-
tops to supply the small chain, Hiller's Markets. "Here I was
making fresh, refrigerated salsa when everybody in the Midwest
ate bottled and pasteurized salsa, if they ate salsa at all."

Jack had found his niche. Then came the tough part: filling it.
Over the next two years, he took several crucial steps that made
his salsa one of the top-selling fresh salsas in the country, and
grew his revenues from $4,000 in 1998 to $12 million in 2004.

Part of what drove this huge spike in revenue was the fact that,
in order for Jack to keep making his product with fresh ingredients
and turn a profit, he had to sell a lot of salsa. If he didn't expand his
reach, he'd need to raise his prices. Jack wasn't comfortable raising
his prices, as he knew any increase could cut back on demand. He
couldn't risk a drop in sales—what made Jack's Special so attractive
to grocers is that it didn't stay on the shelves very long.

Jack knew he needed to expand, but expansion was slow going.
"Eventually, I was selling to 70 grocery stores carrying my products, but I needed a whole lot more. So I'd show up at a small or
midsized grocery store with five or six pints of salsa. The managers
would usually tell me they didn't like salsas. I left the samples any-
way. You could see somebody throwing out one pint, but not five
or six. I knew they'd have to open them up and share them."

Invariably, the managers would call back and ask him to come
back with a few cases. But he still wasn't getting into the big food
chains that would give him enough volume to make his salsas
profitable.

So in 1999, Jack decided to enter his salsa in the Fiery Food Show in Albuquerque as a way to get in front of regional and national grocery chains. "I figured I'd take a few honorable mentions and sign up a few stores." Amid a field of 350 competing salsas, Jack's Special swept the awards.

Those awards were the turning point for Jack and his little Ferndale firm. Five years after winning first place at the Fiery Food Show, Jack's products (now expanded to a dozen different salsas, chips, and dips like spinach-cheese) are in 35 states and 4,000 stores. In 2002, the company changed its name from Jack's Garden Fresh Salsa to Garden Fresh Gourmet. But the ideals behind the company haven't changed at all. Jack still samples his products extensively, continually converting new consumers without spending any money on big advertising campaigns. He employs nine full-time employees whose only job is to travel the country checking out the company's refrigerated displays, cleaning them up, and opening up pint after pint of salsa and tearing open bags of chips for people to taste. And he never scrimps on quality, even if it means scouring the country for ways to make a fresh guacamole that doesn't need any preservatives. "People [thought I was] a lunatic trying to make fresh guacamole, but I'm selling more of it than anybody else now." He found that you could seal the guacamole under ultrahigh pressure to kill off the yeast that makes avocados brown. The only thing that's in Jack's guacamole is avocado, onion, cilantro, and jalapeños. That's the essence of Jack's business in a pint of guacamole: clean, fresh ingredients with no preservatives.

Key Moves

1. **Getting in the Mix.** In order for Jack to have his *ah-hah!* moments, he had to raise his awareness level and learn more about opportunities in the market. His breakthrough ideas came to him when he was at trade shows picking up on trends and customer reactions.

2. **Getting Feedback.** Jack got smart by testing the product with customers before investing heavily—he started by offering his salsa in only one retail location so he could get feedback from customers and refine his recipes. He used that feedback to get a sense of what the market demand would be. He also used the positive response from those initial customers to convince other grocery stores to sell his product.

3. **Finding a Niche.** There were established salsa brands already filling the shelves at grocery stores. So Jack created a distinctly different *fresh* product that would be located in a separate part of the store—the refrigerated section. He had found a way to create a unique niche within the salsa industry, in terms of both product and placement.

4. **Keeping the Spirit.** Jack stayed close to the front lines of his business and continues to interact with customers to this day. He conducts taste tests and works up new recipes constantly. He's as involved in his business today as he was when he was just getting started as a salsa entrepreneur. This also goes back to Key Move #1, "Getting in the Mix," which allows Jack to adjust his products and strategies in an ever-changing marketplace.

5. **Pricing.** Jack found—and stuck to—a sweet spot in the minds of consumers. He offered a premium product at only a slightly higher price point than the processed salsas. While his per-unit sales were less profitable than they could have been, he was able to sell a lot more product in total. The result: higher volumes, a much bigger share of the market, and meteoric growth in revenues.

6. **Grassroots Marketing.** Having a presence at the trade shows, conducting taste tests, winning awards, and promoting his successes through the media have proven to be low-priced but priceless marketing strategies for Jack. It's allowed him to keep his advertising budgets low while still positively influencing consumers and grocers.

CHAPTER EIGHT

Get Ready! Get Set!

The First 12 Months—
a Survival Guide

This coming year—your first year in business—will be filled with hard work, long nights, and many frustrations. In equal or greater measure, this year will overflow with thrilling moments, personal triumphs, and a level of satisfaction we know you'd never achieve working for somebody else.

We should know. We've been through this "first year" dozens of times with our own businesses. We've coached many others through these critical months, too. The first year is one of our favorite stages in the life of a business. We savor the late nights when we can't stop thinking about the business, what needs to be done that moment, and what needs to be done the next day. The line between success and failure is at its thinnest.

We're energized knowing that every little move we make in the early stage of a business is critical to its ultimate success; every dime spent counts; every new hire has to be the best; every new customer further fuels the fires; and every strategic decision can take us down a road to victory or a road to doom. Realizing how each day will make a difference, we arrive at work with a singular sense of purpose and focus that's unique to this early stage of running a business.

From those experiences, we've learned a couple of important lessons we recommend you adopt to make your first year in business one of the best years of your life. First, *work from the heart*. When you do so, you'll stay in tune with your dreams and goals. The reason you're starting this business probably isn't that you like charting your debt-to-equity ratios or taking inventory on a Saturday morning. You're doing this because you're *passionate* about starting something of your own, creating your own success, and seeing your ideas or inventions blossom into a real, thriving business that benefits your customers. Maintaining that passion and excitement is essential during the first year of business. One of the best ways to do this is to pull out your Life Plan and remind yourself why you started up this business in the first place.

Second, *keep your mind in the game*. This is all about having mastery of the vital stats of your business. Each day, check on key functions in your business. This includes things like your financial performance, staff performance, sales performance, and whatever other important factors drive your business to success or failure. Keeping close tabs on these areas can provide you with early warning signs that will give you time to take action before things go completely awry.

By following this "heart and mind" wisdom, we've been able to strike a balance between the hard work and the true enjoyment that comes from entrepreneurship. We'll be the first to admit, however, that it can be a tough balancing act. We've had our moments of being far too excited about a project and failing to see that our burn rate was too high, that we were over budget. There've been other times when we got so bogged down in just trying to make the business work that we ended up bummed out and burned out.

But during the past few years, we've become better at this balancing act by clearly defining what we need to do every day to keep the business humming along and to keep our excitement high. Now we'd like to share these ideas with you.

Five Things to Help You Succeed

This list helps keep our heads clear about our business no matter how fast-paced things get. In the list, we coach you on taking risks, keeping the entrepreneurial spirit alive, innovating, working hard but working smart, and managing your burn rate. Each item on the list offers actionable strategies that you can use to keep your new business on track.

1. Be bold.

By nature, entrepreneurs are risk-takers. Even so, as your business gets into a rhythm, you might find yourself falling into the trap of taking fewer and fewer risks, opting instead for what's familiar, stable, and routine. If this happens, you've got to get back in touch with the boldness that got your business off the ground in the first place. Just because you're on your way doesn't mean you can put your business on cruise control. If you do, you may find yourself losing out on an opportunity and losing passion for what you do. One of the best ways to get *and stay* ahead is to keep taking risks. Not careless and reckless ones, but calculated, sensible risks that draw upon your strengths and lead you closer to your ultimate objectives.

We've been bold and have taken many risks in our two decades of running companies. One of the most outlandish, but also most worthwhile, was when we got into the business of selling juggling balls.

In 1992, the Battery Buddy was just hitting the market. We were traveling to Sears stores across the country to train their salespeople on how to promote and sell the product. But no royalty checks were streaming in yet—that would take a good six months—and we needed cash flow *that* month. So instead of kicking back and waiting for the Battery Buddy proceeds, we kicked into gear and began hunting for a way to generate some cash flow in the interim.

One weekend, as part of our national tour to train Sears personnel on how to sell the Battery Buddy, we found ourselves at a Sears store in Miami's Aventura Mall. We had finished a very trying training session and were walking through the mall's main atrium to the other side where our car was parked. As we rounded a corner, we happened upon a woman selling juggling balls from one of those pushcarts you see in many malls.

We stopped to take a look.

The juggling kit's brand name caught our attention. "More Balls Than Most." We liked the cheekiness of the brand. The name seemed to apply to us, given how we'd ultimately triumphed with the Battery Buddy invention despite all the setbacks over the years. So we stopped for a lesson in juggling.

She told us—as she taught us to juggle—that she was helping her friends in London, England, sell their juggling kits but that she was having a hard time finding distribution for the product. Most juggling balls are pretty cheap and inexpensive. But More Balls Than Most comes in a beautiful leatherette box, with a clever manual rich with British humor, and the balls themselves had a tactile feel to them that we later called the *oooh!* factor. They retailed for $19.95.

Initially, we agreed with the woman that it seemed like a tough sell, but as we juggled we realized there was more to this than just a casual game. We'd come out of Sears a bit stressed and tired from our cross-country tour. The juggling had taken our minds off of our exhaustion, and we found ourselves smiling and laughing.

That's when the lightbulb switched on for both of us. If we could figure out a way to market More Balls Than Most as a fun, interesting way to relieve stress, then we could command a higher price for the juggling set closer to $29.95. If we could do that, then we would, by accident, have happened onto another business that could pay the bills while we waited for our royalty checks from Masco. Of course, it would be a big risk. What did we know about how to sell juggling kits for stress relief? Further, we had no preexisting distribution and we had a negligible marketing budget.

But we had faith in that *ah-hah!* moment, and we followed through on our instinct. Less than a month later, we received our first container load of juggling kits shipped by sea from England. Awaiting that shipment, we had already started taking meetings, and as we'd anticipated, started taking orders from buyers at the high-end retailers. They loved More Balls Than Most! By 1993, we'd secured the exclusive United States distributor rights for the product. That year, Rich taught thousands of people to juggle—customers and salespeople alike—at Neiman-Marcus, Marshall Field's, Saks Fifth Avenue, Nordstrom, and Dillard's stores across the country. More Balls Than Most became one of that year's best-selling Father's Day gifts.

It was an extraordinary success for us. It was also a shining example of what can happen when you maintain that bold and willful spirit that puts you on the entrepreneurial path in the first place. We were willing to do whatever it took to get off of the peanut-butter-and-jelly budget and make our business take flight, even if it entailed yet another huge risk. Being bold and taking smart risks can do the same for you.

2. Keep the entrepreneurial spirit alive.

There's nothing more damaging to a business than the lack of entrepreneurial spirit. Businesses, especially small businesses, depend on a constant infusion of new ideas and energy. It's easy to have ideas and energy when you're first starting up. You might be one of the millions who've been thinking up great ideas for years before you decided to open for business. But as your business matures—even just six months out of the gate—it can become more and more difficult to keep that entrepreneurial spirit alive. That's especially true if you're successful. The irony is that success is often the enemy of entrepreneurial spirit. You're forging ahead with the business, the cash flow looks good, you've got happy employees, and the customers keep coming back. There's less and less need to be entrepreneurial and more and more of a tendency to focus solely on procedures. We've had this happen to us any number of times. But we've learned to manage these success sinkholes with a few exercises that recharge the entrepreneurial batteries.

- **Jump-start the vision:** Some of our best ideas occur when we're far away. It's not always easy to take time away from the office, but we force ourselves to do it because we realize that we must keep innovating, and we must keep the vision for the company fresh and exciting. It's hard to do that while you're concentrating on routine things such as office management or personnel problems. We've learned it's important to plan employee retreats away from the office, too, so we can all brainstorm together. And while we sometimes find ourselves putting in long hours in the evenings or on weekends, it's equally important to take some evenings and weekends away from the business. Remember to spend time with family and friends and take time to enjoy your other interests. You'll find that if you force yourself to do these things, you'll be rewarded with your best and most innovative ideas.

    You don't have to choose a minivacation to recharge the batteries. What's important is finding activities that help you reignite that fire in the belly you had when you first started.

Think back to the early days of starting your business, or even before that when you were still dreaming of owning your own company. Is there one thing that you used to do that got you psyched up about the business?

- **Communicate the vision:** Once you've recharged and returned to the office with fresh thinking, communicate your new vision to your team. Seek their input and buy-in as well. You may be the first one to have the entrepreneurial spirit, but your team members are going to be the ones who help refine the vision for the company and help put any new ideas into action.

- **Create a culture of entrepreneurship:** To encourage employees to act like entrepreneurs, reward radical thinking. This can be tough, especially when your business is on its way to being successful. You don't want *anything* to upset that. But as testimony to the power of encouraging entrepreneurship within your organization, we recall a radio show we broadcasted from center stage at the Los Angeles Fortune Small Business "Go for Growth" Conference in August 2004. We had assembled a panel of Super Startup entrepreneurs on the show, including Lavetta Willis, who runs Dada Footwear, which we discussed in Chapter One. A gentleman from the audience asked Lavetta, "How do you deal with change in the marketplace?" Without a pause, Lavetta leaned forward in her seat and said softly, "At our company, we don't deal with change, we create it." She indicated that in her organization they try to stay ahead of the curve. Lavetta focuses on creating a culture of entrepreneurship where radical thinking and risk-taking are not only encouraged but expected. This culture has been a key part of her company's success.

Here are additional tips to help you invigorate the entrepreneurial spirit:

- **Stamp out the 9-to-5 mentality.** Employees who see their work as "just a job" can destroy the spirit you're seeking. The single most effective way we've found to stamp out this "job" mentality is to think of your company as a pie with entrepreneurship as the filling. Then imagine cutting up the pie and serving each of your employees their own piece. By giving each of them a piece of the business, you turn employees into entrepreneurs themselves. The more responsibility they have to make decisions about what needs to be done, the more they'll take ownership of the fate of your company.

- **Organize the org chart.** One of the quickest ways to decide if you've given employees enough responsibility is to revisit your organization's structure, usually distilled into a hierarchical block diagram called an org chart. If you're still operating a business with only a few people, determine what responsibilities each employee has. Do this with the knowledge that defining roles and responsibilities and reporting more clearly will actually create clarity and opportunities for creativity.

  We're not advocating hierarchy or unnecessary structure. On the contrary, we just want you to consciously establish an organizational structure that works for *your* business and what *you* want to achieve.

  (Note: When you organize your company structure, make sure not to distance yourself from front-line employees. Avoid unnecessary layers.)

- **Remember to reward entrepreneurial behavior.** Channel your employees' entrepreneurial drive by outlining the goals for their project or activity. Determine with the employee what those goals should be. If they reach those goals, then reward them—entrepreneurial spirit will wither without this incentive. The rewards will link responsibility with accountability as you're infusing your employees with entrepreneurial spirit.

  Also, be creative! The rewards don't have to be monetary—they can be as simple as recognizing achievements of one person in front of a group. It could be lunch with the boss or a few extra days off.

3. Keep innovating by listening to customers and tracking competitors.

• **Let the market tell you what it wants.** We're not the first ones to say it, but we're true believers that it's critical for you to listen to your existing and prospective customers. The closer you are to your market, the better equipped you are to take that entrepreneurial spirit you've pumped up inside your company and channel it into real products and services that crank up the profits. Avoid the common pitfall of innovating without receiving feedback from the market. Far too often passion can get the best of us, and entrepreneurs end up thinking they already know what the market wants. But it's terribly dangerous to make key decisions in a vacuum. It's equally dangerous to make decisions based on very limited market feedback. Doing so can give you a false sense of confidence, leading you to think you understand what the market really wants, where they want to buy it, at what price they become a customer, and so on. Just think what a shame it would be if you committed to production or even printing brochures and only then found out that the market actually wanted a *different* product or service at a *different* price point.

You'll learn more about how important this topic is to us later when we discuss a concept called the "CEOs of Communication." But you can be sure we're always listening to our customers—the citizens of the StartupNation community who look to us for answers and advice for their businesses. We hear from them on the radio, through our website and online seminars, and at the conferences we attend around the country. We listen closely to them not only to address their direct questions but because their input helps us streamline our overall products and services. Some of the best features and aspects of StartupNation have come from this kind of dialogue. Here's just one example:

When we launched our website, we began offering online seminars every Wednesday. We coined the seminars "Webinar Wednesdays." It was an efficient way to meet up with our community by inviting them to join in via the Internet and a toll-free call to learn about a new topic each week. One week was financing, the next week we'd jump to franchising, then marketing, and so on. Each subject was important in its own right and things were going well.

Then we noticed an important phenomenon. Attendance was hovering around the same level from week to week, and there were only a low number of repeat attendees. We were perplexed. So during the webinars each week, we began announcing that we were interested in finding out what attendees wanted to hear about in upcoming sessions. More often than not, they responded with a desire to learn something *more* about whatever topic we were covering that day. We realized that our customers were seeking a lot more detail than we were providing. To dive deeper, we came up with a simple (and now obvious) solution. We began offering series of webinars that had continuity from week to week. For one month straight, we would cover finance. Then we would do a run of webinars on marketing, and so on. And *voilà*! Familiar names started appearing in our registrations. People began signing up with consistency each week. Registration started growing, and the percentage of repeat visitors has since skyrocketed.

By listening to our customers, we were able to create the exact service they were looking for. Had we not listened, in spite of our best in-office thinking, the online seminar series would eventually have gone by the wayside. Some of the best innovations, we've learned, are conceived when you listen closely to what the market screams for.

- **Watch the competition:** While listening to your customers is paramount in business, it's also valuable to watch the competition. Competition is a given, and the better the business opportunity, the more you'll face. To stay ahead, make sure you keep your eye on them. There's nothing wrong with learning from your competition, not for the purpose of copycatting, but so that you can measure how you're doing relative to them. If you pay attention, you'll learn from mistakes they're making, at their expense, and you'll learn where they might be succeeding in ways that you aren't. And then you can adapt accordingly.

It's always better to have your competition chasing you than you chasing them. And the best way to stay ahead is by continuing to innovate. Markets mature over time, novelty wears off, what was once considered fresh and exciting becomes a commodity, and as a result, many businesses that don't stay ahead of the competition are forced to compete simply on price. No doubt better pricing can definitely be a competitive advantage; but beware of competing only on price. Not only will someone else certainly come along and beat your price at some point, lowering your prices will cut into your margins and ultimately lead to a less profitable business. Don't let this happen to you. One way to keep that from happening is to continue to innovate.

Be innovative about product and service offerings, both new and existing; innovate new ways of marketing; innovate faster and more efficient ways of distribution. If you innovate often, maintain high quality and functionality for your products, and create cachet through clever marketing, you may even be able to raise your prices above the competition without losing customers.

4. Work hard *and* work smart.

It's been said that running your own business is like running a marathon at a sprint pace. Research does show that entrepreneurs work longer hours than salaried employees. And it's true that hard work is essential to achieving entrepreneurial success. But hard work isn't enough. You must also work "smart." We've learned that an hour of quality work is better than a day of mediocre work. It's more about the quality than the quantity.

- **Take 5 at Night and 10 in the Morning:** The worst thing that can happen to a business is "drift." If there were laws of physics that applied to entrepreneurship, the "inevitability of drift" would be one of them. Drift occurs naturally when you become so embroiled in your day-to-day work that you don't really know where your business is headed. We understand that in a small business pretty much everything seems important or urgent at some point. But drift is not a matter of whether you're working on important things, it's a matter of whether you're working on *the most important* things.

You know you're experiencing drift if you have difficulty answering the following questions without hesitation: What are your goals for your business? What are your top three priorities for the month ahead? What are your top priorities for the week ahead? For today? Without complete command of answers to these questions, you risk floating adrift in your business, and wasting money and time in the process.

Fixing the drift problem is easy. It literally can take a painless 5 minutes at the end of the day and another 10 minutes or so the next morning. At night, before you leave your office, take five minutes to reflect on the day. What didn't I get done? What should I do first tomorrow? Is there anything I'm leaving undone that's going to keep me awake? The next morning, take action on the reflections of the night before. Whether you keep an actual "to-do list" or keep track of issues in your head, the mornings are a perfect time to prioritize the day's work, putting at the top of the list any of the business fundamentals that you need to focus on that day. By thinking strategically about the business every day—how are our people doing? are the financials looking good this week?—we keep our business on track instead of letting it drift.

- **Weekends Away:** The daily "5 and 10" method can be effective, but, sometimes you need more than this daily fix. Even though you've been taking action and getting the work done, bigger issues can sneak up. Are you meeting your expectations in terms of both the business and life? Are there any serious management problems that you need to address that you haven't dealt with on your daily to-do list? Have customer complaints started piling up, or have sign-ups to the website been down for a few months? If you start to feel that the daily checkup isn't keeping you on track, take the weekend off and pull out your Life Plan and business plan. Do this just as you would take a minivacation to think of ways to innovate. But this time, think about things like: Are you working your Life Plan as well as your business plan? Is there something in the business plan that you've forgotten, a nugget of information or wisdom that you thought of when you wrote it that could help you now? Are your financials on track with the money plan you put in place? Sometimes a needed change can be as simple as considering a new software system to keep better track of your company's finances. Or it can be as critical as realizing that you aren't meeting the Life Plan goals you laid out and that it's time to make changes to fix what's derailing you. This checking in, which we do at least every six months, is critical because the longer you let your company drift, the harder it is to put it back on track.

- **Delegate early and often.** Trying to do everything is a fatal mistake made by many entrepreneurs. Somehow you must break away from the common attitude that you're the only one who can do it right. If you've built the right team around you and soberly assessed your strengths and weaknesses, passions and

QUICK TIP

Don't Micromanage

When delegating, you must entrust the person to do the job right.

Set clear expectations and get status reports regularly. Provide guidance but do not hover over the person's shoulder constantly. Your people will stop thinking for themselves if you constantly think for them.

priorities, delegating will amplify—not hamper—your company's performance. Further, it will allow you to focus on the things you love, leading you to greater satisfaction and energy.

No matter what, as your business ramps up, you'll deal with bigger and bigger demands on your time. To counter this, consider another type of delegating called "outsourcing." Outsourcing can be useful when you've identified activities in your business that take up precious time and human resources but aren't necessarily central to the value you provide your customers. Examples are functions like bookkeeping, accounting, and management of your information technology (your company's software and hardware). Some businesses can even outsource operational components such as manufacturing and fulfillment—the packaging and shipping of your product. Sales through independent rep firms would also fall into this category. Each of these may be better handled by other organizations while you focus entirely on the most strategic aspects of your business, whatever you deem them to be. At first the concept of delegating these functions to outside vendors may feel scary or may sound pricey, but if you do your research, get plenty of references, and institute a disciplined management process for these relationships, you'll find you'll have more time to be the entrepreneur that's so critical to your business's success.

- **Get rid of inefficiency.** Often when you're just starting up, you don't think too much about how efficient your business is, you just want to get it up and running. But by going back into the business every few months and checking where you're being inefficient, you can reenergize your company. Consider the technology you're using. And what about your system for production, inventory, and distribution? Do you have the right people on board?

  Let's say you're an eBay seller with a solid list of customers and orders growing every day. At first, you're easily able to pack and ship all the products yourself and maintain those high seller scores on eBay that keep people coming back to you. But as the business grows, you find yourself packing shipments when you should be scouting for new merchandise, wrapping packages at midnight, and racing to meet shipment times. What's truly the best way for you to spend your time? It could be appropriate to consider hiring an extra person or enlisting the help of a child or other relative. You could even try out one of the new pack-and-ship companies that have started up to serve eBay sellers around the country.

One simple way to strike out inefficiency is to take a look at how you deal with inventory. This might not seem applicable to all businesses—especially people in the service sector or knowledge businesses like consulting—but in fact it is. Your inventory is your current amount of the thing you sell— whether it's salsa or books or your time and expertise as a consultant. You don't want that inventory to collect dust. So first take a look at how long it takes you to "turn over" inventory— the term for emptying your warehouse or store of your stocked goods. The more rapidly you buy and sell your inventory, the more profitable you'll be. If your inventory turnover rates are lower than standard for your industry, take measures to move inventory faster, take on less inventory, or, even better, find a way to have others hold the inventory for you. You could negotiate what are called "drop shipments," inventory that is delivered only when you need it.

Don't forget to look at your production and distribution for inefficiencies and unneeded complexity. Complexity is the undisputed enemy in a small business. You may have chosen certain types of production and distribution when you first started because they were readily available. But now that you're growing, you should rethink your production methods. For instance, if you're using a contract manufacturer to make your products, check in every so often to see if you could get a better deal if you went to a larger production run. Remember, Cheryl Tallman of Fresh Baby was able to reduce the costs of her plastic trays by deciding on a larger production run, although she knew in the beginning she wouldn't be selling 50,000 trays a year.

Distribution is also key to efficiency. Many business owners start out as their own distributors, driving hundreds of miles to stock stores because that's the easiest way to get shelf space. It may be easy, but it might not be the most cost-effective method in the long run. Check your distribution system against other systems. Run the numbers to see if you'd be better off hiring a broker who could put you into more and larger stores.

Finally, invest in the right technology to help you collect, measure, and analyze your business fundamentals. The brilliant thing about living in the twenty-first century is that there's a plethora of technology available at really low prices to help businesses perform better. You'll find that sales-analysis software or customer-relationship-management software (which helps you track and manage your interactions with customers) will pay for itself by helping you understand your business better and make important tactical decisions to position you for success.

- **Remember the CEOs of Communication:** The simple act of talking can be a great way to help you work smarter. From conversations with your customers to staff meetings with your employees, communications can help you attack problems before they become intractable and can help you take the daily psychic temperature of your business. We practice the "CEOs of Communication" because there are three groups of people you should be talking to on a regular basis to help you work smarter.

First, C is for customers. To really understand how you're doing out there on "Main Street," we strongly encourage you to talk with some of your important customers about their degree of satisfaction and their recommendations for what you sell. The last thing you want is for your next communication with a customer to be a complaint. More often than not, sloppy entrepreneurs lose a customer before ever knowing the customer was angry or disgruntled. So be proactive. Pick up the phone if it's appropriate. Start an e-mail list to stay in touch. Send out promotions to repeat customers. Poll them informally when they're on the premises. These little efforts can pay off big time, especially if you are competing against big corporations. Relationships are what keep people coming back to small businesses, so nurture your customers. You'll learn, you'll impress them, and you won't have to waste precious time trying to win them back.

Employees are the E in CEO. There's nothing harder to do as a boss than stamp out gossip about the business or put people back on track about the strategic vision of the company. To work smarter, communicate early and often with employees. We find that many small businesses think they're "too small" to worry about communicating formally with employees. They assume that news, initiatives, and priorities will somehow work their way through the office. But weekly meetings can go a long way in creating a work environment where employees know what's on the mind of management and where the company is headed.

Finally, there's the O, for owners. Not all of you will have shareholders or stakeholders to worry about, but many of you will—owners can be your friends and family who invested a few thousand dollars with you, all the way up to venture capitalists who are helping you through your third round of financing. When it comes to communicating with this group, we advise *against* delegating. You should personally let the owners know where the business stands financially. Be candid and direct. Even if the news isn't rosy, whatever it is will get out at some point; better you deliver the news than the owners hear it through the grapevine. These communications can go a long way in managing the expectations of your shareholders and create confidence in the business.

For all of these communications, we suggest setting up a regular schedule on your calendar so you don't forget to take the time to talk.

5. Constantly manage your burn rate.

As children, we learned to sail on the Great Lakes. You can sail for days without sight of land on these big, freshwater lakes. With their beauty, though, comes the reality that those waters can also be treacherous. So as trained sailors, we would never think of leaving port for an extended cruise without a clear idea of where we were headed, aided by frequent checks of the compass to make certain we were on course.

We think the same philosophy applies in business. We would never step into a business without having a good handle on its financial fundamentals, and that means having firm control on the company's burn rate.

Simply put, your burn rate is how much capital you're burning through each month. When you start up, you begin with a specific amount of capital (either invested or loaned to the business)—let's say $100,000 as an easy example. You decide that it takes $10,000 a month to operate your business, with no revenues projected during the first year. That means your burn rate is $10,000 a month, and in this example you'd be in trouble if you don't have plans to start making money by your tenth month in business.

The burn rate calculation gets more interesting when revenues start coming in. Back to our example: If you project that in month six you'll start earning $5,000 a month, then your burn rate drops from $10,000 a month to $5,000 a month, even though your operating expenses have stayed steady at $10,000 per month. To calculate your monthly burn rate, subtract revenues earned from expenses incurred during the month. What you're shooting for is to have no burn rate at all. That occurs when, in any given month, you make more than you spend.

Knowing your burn rate and managing it well will tell you—and indicate to your investors—just how long it will take to "burn" through your money before you need additional investment or a loan or until you will break even and begin to make a profit. If you forget to check this compass within your business, you could burn through your cash before you reach these milestones and find yourself out of business. Always remember that cash is one of the most precious resources in your company, in addition to your employees and customers. A business simply cannot operate without cash.

To make certain you have that precious resource on hand, watch the most important component of the burn rate equation: your expenses. While you need review your burn rate only every month, you need to monitor how much money you spend every day.

The easiest thing to remember when deciding whether to spend the money or not is this: Will this expenditure help the company become profitable more quickly, and will it help me get to the next milestone in my business? For example, consider the difference between spending money on a new shipment of inventory you know customers will go crazy for versus buying gorgeous new office furniture that makes you feel good. We've found that one of the best ways to think through expenses is to take a day to reflect. We ask, Is the product or service critical to our business? Then we make the decision the next day on whether to spend the money or not.

Build Equity to Sell Well

When you're just starting up, it seems almost ludicrous to think about selling your business. But if you've followed the advice we provided on life planning and business planning, you probably have a sense of what your desired endgame is. Here we point out some of the ways you can build value into your business if you intend to sell it someday.

Exit strategies can take a variety of forms. You can sell your assets piecemeal. Alternatively, you can sell the company to internal management or you can choose to shift operational responsibility to them and remain involved as a passive owner. Another exit strategy you might consider is selling your business.

Potential Buyers for Your Business
- A company in a different niche that wants access to yours.
- A dead-on competitor who wants to remove the threat you represent.
- A company seeking your distribution, premium shelf space, relationships and/or location.
- A consolidator rolling multiple companies into a conglomerate.

Selling your business down the road for a handsome sum requires strategic planning and execution at the outset. Maximize the value of your company by evaluating assets you already have or can create over time.

Strategies to Optimize the Value of Your Business
- Develop a committed and capable team that could continue on with the business after the sale.
- Build solid relationships with vendors, retailers, and customers.

- Establish customers and contracts that generate recurring revenue.
- Develop a marching brand. Again and again, companies have built immense value by establishing strong name recognition.
- Develop a portfolio of proprietary products and the patents and trademarks that protect them.
- Avoid overburdening your business with debt. You want to keep a "clean balance sheet," which limits the amount of debt to an optimal level.
- Take a lower salary over the course of time. Instead of milking company profits along the way, plow profits back into the company in order to position yourself for a bigger payoff at exit.

As you ponder your exit strategy, remember to keep a set of well-organized financial records. This is always important, but it becomes *critical* if you plan to sell. The due diligence conducted by a company interested in buying your business will be very thorough. They'll look into the books like you look back at your childhood diary, discovering the history and true performance of your past. Any weaknesses in accounting or record keeping will undermine value during final negotiations.

CHAPTER NINE

OPEN FOR BUSINESS

What Does Success Mean to You?

By reading this book, we hope you've replaced confusion with knowledge; replaced fear with confidence. Now it's time to replace dreaming with doing. There's no better time than *now* to start up your business. You'll never be better positioned to take that first step toward creating your dream business and living the life you've always wanted. So don't wait until tomorrow or next week to get started. Do something now that takes you one step closer to becoming the owner of your own business and the architect of your own life.

Don't squander this opportunity to do something you've always wanted to do. Don't put this book on the shelf and let it gather dust. Don't let anything stand in your way, because we know starting your own business is one of the most powerful and meaningful things you'll do in your life. It's a way for you to achieve success.

And remember, don't be limited by the stereotypical measure of success—how rich you become. That's certainly not how we measure success. *It's not about the money!* Instead, what keeps us enthusiastic and energetic are the key elements in our StartupNation Manifesto—work as freedom, work as family, and work as fulfillment.

Success for us is having the *freedom* to work according to our own schedules with our own roles, rules, and responsibilities, defined by our own sense of what's important.

Now, of course, we recognize that making money is important—obviously, it's fundamental. And no doubt there are privileges that come with financial success, and there's nothing wrong with that! But for us, money is just a means to an end. It's the currency that enables us to enjoy the freedom that we find so important. To be specific, we're talking about the freedom to set our own schedule instead of punching a time card; to work when we want and play when we want; to *choose* the number of hours we work each day. Instead of taking orders from a boss, we come up with our own strategies and take initiative. We're energized by running our own show, being responsible for our own successes, and being accountable for our own failures.

Success for us is making sure our business has a *family* spirit. As in any strong family, the individuals who are part of our business family contribute to a greater whole. The individuals feel that they "belong," that they have a bond with the rest of the team. We share common values and goals, support each other through times of challenge, and celebrate each other's triumphs. Whether it's the two of us working together as brothers or ensuring that our employees feel they're part of a close-knit familial team, we've witnessed how powerful the family spirit can be for a company. And others have, too.

One such entrepreneur we've known for years is Dan Gilbert, founder and chairman of Quicken Loans. Dan started his mortgage business in 1985, when he was just 23. Today he leads the company's 2,250 "team members." In 2003, Quicken Loans was recognized as the nation's leading online retail mortgage lender, closing more than $12 billion in loans, and *Fortune* magazine named Quicken Loans one of the "Best Places to Work" in its annual list of great companies to work for. This is reflective of Dan's philosophy to create a family atmosphere at work.

"With this company, more than anything I wanted to create a culture of ownership in which each of our team members has a voice," Dan says of his philosophy to foster teamwide pride in the company. And that's not an easy thing to do when your team grows as quickly as Dan's has. Among the tactics Dan has used to accomplish his goal, he developed Quicken Loans "Isms" that capture the company's core philosophies and guiding principles. The Isms are distributed at new-team-member orientations and displayed on posters throughout the office hallways. Here are a few:

- *Innovation is rewarded. Execution is worshiped.*
- *Every Client. Every Time. No Exception. No Excuse.*
- *You'll See It When You Believe It*
- *Always Raising Our "Level of Awareness"*

Dan has created a unique culture that fosters creativity and new ideas. He expects team members to assume responsibility and take the initiative to make something better. There's an open-door policy to communication at Quicken Loans, including monthly team meetings, CEO e-mails, rallies, annual company meetings and an intranet site that encourages employees to write up their ideas.

Quicken Loans has also built a reward program into its culture, including bonuses, gift certificates, and vacations to exciting destinations to recognize great performance. But beyond the more typical incentive programs, the company sets a welcoming tone by having regular employee meetings at which Quicken Loans' in-house rock band—Rate Lock—plays. And just like a real family, the company sends hand-signed birthday cards to team members and sends their children gift certificates for their birthdays. During peak periods, such as a refinancing boom, the Quicken Loans family is served meals for free in the company cafeteria. Bringing everyone together for lunch gives people a chance to exchange ideas in an informal setting and fosters a team culture.

As consuming as managing Quicken Loans may sound, Dan is now building up yet another "extended family." As this book goes to print, he has fulfilled his lifelong dream of owning a professional sports team by purchasing the NBA's Cleveland Cavaliers. And in Dan's first public announcement about the transaction, he stressed—you guessed it—that he plans to lead his basketball organization "with a team-oriented philosophy to achieve maximum potential" just as he does at Quicken Loans.

It's clear that for Dan—as it is for us—creating family spirit is integral to his success.

Success for us means being *fulfilled* by the work we do. It's more than just about "getting by"—it's about the fulfillment that comes from confronting a challenge and overcoming it. It's about the fulfillment that comes from seeing what was once just an idea start selling like hotcakes. It's about the fulfillment from knowing that the work we do has a profoundly positive impact on people within and outside the walls of our office. That's one of the reasons why we founded StartupNation. We wanted to help entrepreneurs achieve their dreams.

Rich

We have a feature on the radio show called "The Hook Up," where we link an entrepreneur with a decision maker who otherwise would be difficult to reach. For someone seeking retail distribution, we might hook them up with a buyer from Target. Or we might find an infomercial producer for someone who wants to sell on TV. We invite the decision maker to come on the air with us and listen to a pitch from the entrepreneur. If there's interest, we help them continue their discussion off-air, which hopefully results in a fruitful relationship between the parties. We've done this successfully several times on the show. When it happens, we're out of our seats jumping

up and down, because it's such a rush to fulfill our mission of
helping someone get closer to achieving their goals.

There are many ways to be fulfilled through entrepreneurship.
The beauty is that you can set your own definition of what fulfills
you. It might be simple. It might be grand. It doesn't matter what
it is as long as it's something that's personally important to you.
One entrepreneur very recently affirmed our belief that business
gives you a path to personal fulfillment. His name is Mike
Korchinsky. We interviewed him on our radio show and find his
story unforgettable.

After Mike had sold his successful management consultancy in
1995, he decided to reward himself with a trip he had always
dreamed of—he went on safari in Kenya. While there, he ended
up taking a side trip to a nearby village where, he was told, sus-
pected poachers lived. "Instead of seeing a gang of seedy guys
with eye patches—my idea of a band of poachers—I saw a village
with 5,000 people, families, women, and children."

It was during that village trip that Mike started thinking about
a way to save animals from the poachers while also changing the
lives of the villagers who hunted them. That vision has become a
reality in his company, Wildlife Works, which he started 18
months after his Kenyan safari. The basics of the company are
simple. Today, shirts, pants, and yogawear are designed in the
United States and are sewn by those same Kenyan villagers. The
clothes are then exported to the United States, to be sold at stores
such as REI and through the company's website, www.wildlife-
works.com. Now, instead of poaching, the Kenyan villagers are
growing cotton and making T-shirts that display the images of the
animals—the same animals they once would have killed in order
to sell their pelts and tusks on the black market.

Wildlife Works makes its mission a selling point, notifying American consumers exactly where the clothes are made, how many jobs

they're supporting, and how much money the villagers make. His clothing factory is built on fair and equitable labor practices.

Consumers are assured that they're helping to preserve animals in Africa with every clothing purchase they make. "The big brand companies have forgotten how much power they have to change a place," Mike says. This "consumer-powered conservation" has helped Mike set aside an 80,000-acre preserve in Kenya. He hopes to buy even more land as the company's sales grow. But Mike isn't the only one holding up his end of the bargain. The Kenyan villagers have stopped poaching and clearing forests now that they realize the well-paying jobs—$50 a week in a country where the average yearly income is $500—aren't going away. Instead, the career opportunities and salaries are growing.

"There's never a better time to lay the groundwork for the social impact you want to make than when you're first starting up a business," he shares. "Startups really are the engine for change—in America, in Africa, anywhere."

Mike and his company are a great example of how a business can profoundly affect people's lives for the better. He's a living example of how a business can nourish the entrepreneur with a degree of fulfillment that's unparalleled.

Live Your Manifesto!

We don't expect that all of you will be driven to change some faraway part of the world like Mike Korchinksy. Perhaps your passion will be better played out on your hometown's Main Street. After all, starting up is all about following through on your own measure of success—be that changing your *own* world or changing the *whole* world. As so many entrepreneurs have told us, including Mike, these personal measures of success are what keep you coming back day after day, year after year, no matter what your business's ups and downs may be.

Whatever your personal and professional reasons for starting up a business, *begin by creating your own manifesto*. For inspiration, look no further than the real-life entrepreneurs we've highlighted throughout this book. Remember Mark Vadon, Scott Kerslake, Kate Richard, Bill MacArthur, Gail Erten, Ray Gunn, Titus Blair, Scott Griggs, Mike Palmer, Lavetta Willis, Dale and Alan Klapmeier, Seth Seaberg and David Young, Joan Isabella, Tom Nardone, the Brady Family, Gretchen Schauffler, Frank Messano, Cheryl Tallman, Jack Aronson, Adam Lowry and Eric Ryan, Peter Romero, Todd Graham and Jonathan Hudson, Patrick Byrne, Carlton Calvin, Phil LaDuca, Ari Weinzweig, Stephanie Odegard, Dan Gilbert, and Mike Korchinksy? Each has an extraordinary story of achievement and is a living example of their own personal manifesto.

Sons and daughters of everyday people, these entrepreneurs are part of a community we call StartupNation. They're people who dream and then pursue their dreams. They know the risks, yet still willingly embrace the challenge. They answer to themselves. And they know there are many meanings to the word "rich."

What stands between you and joining the ranks of this community? Are you ready to hang the sign that tells the world you're "Open for Business"? If we've achieved our primary goal, we've inspired you to *start it up!* We've drawn upon our own and our fellow entrepreneurs' experiences and wisdom to illustrate not only *how* but also *why* to live the life of an entrepreneur. Armed with all of this information and inspiration, now we look forward to having you join us as a full-fledged citizen of StartupNation. Don't wait until tomorrow. Don't put it off.

The time is now.

StartupNation Online

As these chapters end, a new one begins. Set out knowing you're not alone. Connect with us, other entrepreneurs, and the key resources you need to achieve success at www.startupnation.com. There you'll find:

- The online companion to *StartupNation*, **"10 Steps to Open for Business,"** an online tool designed to walk you through the process of starting your own business step by simple step.
- A vibrant **online community** where you can create a profile of you and your business and post questions and answers in the forums.
- **Links** to key resources such as legal forms, loans, angel investors, and more.
- **Online seminars** covering all of the key subjects you need to start and grow your business—including a special series dedicated to inventors.
- Archived **StartupNation Radio shows** that allow you to listen whenever, wherever, and however long you wish. Hear us coach callers on how to make key moves for their businesses.

- A free subscription to our StartupNation **podcasts,** diving deep into advice for entrepreneurs, technology solutions, and Startup-Nation radio shows.
- Archived **Elevator Pitches** that help you learn from the good—and not so good—on-air pitches we've received over the past couple of years.
- Numerous articles about the key moves of **Super Startups** that put them on the path to success.
- How-to articles that give you the inside track on how to raise money, how to market and sell, even how to lead a more balanced life.

By tapping into all of these resources, you'll stay sharp, learn the best practices, and continue to be inspired. Along the way, please drop us an e-mail at sloanbrothers@startupnation.com. Tell us how you're doing. Tell us your story. It's our sincere hope that you'll become a Super Startup like those whose stories we've shared with you in the pages of *StartupNation*.

Index

Jeff Sloan and Rich Sloan
Founders, StartupNation

The founders of StartupNation are venture capitalists, consummate entrepreneurs, and brothers—Jeff and Rich Sloan. The Sloan brothers continue to prove that there's no mountain too high to climb, and as true entrepreneurs they're having a blast along the way.

Jeff and Rich are the perfect role models for budding entrepreneurs. They've faced the many challenges of entrepreneurship and are still creating new businesses every day. Accomplished inventors in their own right, the Sloan brothers have obtained patents for products that have been commercial successes, including the Battery Buddy®, which was licensed and brought to market by a Fortune 500 company. As teenagers, they bought and sold HUD houses. As young adults, they started and sold one of the world's leading Arabian horse-breeding operations, and grew a consumer products import company with best-selling products. In the mid-90s, the Sloan brothers created Sloan Ventures, an early-stage venture development and financing firm that has launched a dozen technology-based businesses.

In 2002, the Sloan brothers created StartupNation to expand their passion for transforming back-of-napkin ideas into real businesses. This fast-growing multi-media company offers entrepreneurs the ultimate resource for living the life they've always dreamed of—by starting their own business. In addition to appearing at events throughout the country, hosting online seminars and providing advice through www.startupnation.com, they're also heard on StartupNation Radio, a nationally syndicated weekend call-in program that offers advice to entrepreneurs in all phases of the business cycle.

Jeff and Rich have been featured on CNN, CNBC, and Fox News Channel and in numerous publications such as the *New York Times,* the *Wall Street Journal, Entrepreneur.com, Inc.,* and *Fortune Small Business.*

The Sloans live their dream of "running their own show" in Birmingham, Michigan.